July 1978

HEALING BY THE SPIRIT

HEALING

BY THE SPIRIT

IVAN COOKE

THE WHITE EAGLE PUBLISHING TRUST
LISS · HAMPSHIRE · ENGLAND
MCMLXXVI

First published in 1955
Revised edition, with new matter, October 1976
.   Copyright © Ivan Cooke 1976

ISBN 0 85487 039 3

Printed in Great Britain by
Fletcher & Son Ltd, Norwich

CONTENTS

Part III
Some Healing Cases

Part I

The Happier Way to Healing

A GLANCE AT THE LESS HAPPY WAY
OF HEALING

In the coming age wisdom as well as knowledge will be restored to man; these will foster a greater concentration on the prevention rather than the cure, of complaints which should never have arisen.

W.E.

Perhaps my first motor-car accident let me off lightly; but the shock and dismay of it happening at all brought me to hospital in rather a stricken state. As I lay in my ward, I felt, let it be confessed, how much more comfortable it might be to shuffle out of this shattered-leg body and take my chance in a next world.

So there I lay in my hospital bed trying to decide whether to go or to stay. Overall I felt detached, neither 'here' nor yet 'there' to any marked extent. Presently it seemed that some effort had to be made, partly for my own sake (one could not just run away) and more so because of those dear to me, and because one had to try to rise above unpleasant things; to put aside, to some degree, awareness of the wardful of patients, the scurrying nurses, the overdriven doctors, the sight of so much sickness in one place. I had resolutely to climb out of the slough of despond if ever I were to recover.

On the whole my thoughts seemed fairly clear. I did not feel too desperately weak. My will to resist became stronger with each effort I made, and so gradually, with daily, hourly effort, I climbed out – or climbed up – and found myself at last safely lodged back on earth; although not too wildly happy, because that 'other place' beyond seemed infinitely more attractive than anything hospital life could offer. Later, lying in my bed, it became clear to me that I had come here to learn something, and learn it I must if the whole experience was not to be wasted. Even a smashed leg might serve some good and useful purpose. Otherwise, why had it happened?

So having little else to do I occupied myself with watching and thinking. I found now that the very novelty and drabness of the hospital ward demanded attention and interest, either directed to this nearby patient or to that, or to the reaction of the several nurses who attended their patients. Both patients and nurses revealed much more of their character than perhaps they were aware. I watched, and noted; not critically but rather to gain appreciation of the value (especially to myself, dependent on it as I was) of the National Health Service responsible for the conditions I was observing.

We have an admirable National Health Service, largely dependent on the good will of those engaged in it. Doctors and nurses have to rise above staleness and chronic tiredness. They have to quell any tendency to become snappy, and remain instead courteous and kind whenever the call comes – and this when often the patient's response invites rebuke.

They were seldom able to stroll or walk around the wards, those nurses (and this would largely apply to the cleaners of wards also, and for that matter to the doctors. They too had little time to spare for pleasantries). The demand was such that they went at a trot rather than a walk. Every duty had to be a hasty duty. Jobs must be scurried through, conversation with patients also. Any friendly feelings must be hurried feelings, and any courtesy expended must be brief. One could not feel that these hospital workers were overpaid, or could ever luxuriate at ease. On the contrary they kept going by a sense of duty, even of dedication – kept going by unflinching will to do so, and in order to be ready for the next job following hard on the heels of the last.

Presently they moved me to another hospital, and then to a third, all within four weeks or so. There seemed little to choose between the three. In each one nurses went at a trot and had progressively less time to stroll or stand around. They all seemed to accept this situation as normal, even natural. All this comes as a tribute to the nursing staff, and indeed to the doctors concerned – of whom I saw little since they had limited time to spare.

I watched the patients as closely as I watched the staff; and with regret saw how often their weakness and boredom during hospital life led to acerbity, to snappiness, to unending demands. At one hospital there was a kind of sun parlour opening up from the ward itself; a pleasant enough place, where patients not bound to their beds might go – men in their sixties and perhaps seventies who must have already decided that they were very old indeed, for they looked vastly older than their age warranted. Once out in this sun parlour (which I soon christened the mausoleum) these 'elderlies' retreated into themselves, into a coma of closed eyes and heavy breathing with seldom a word for anyone. Yet they were never really asleep, nor yet content. No book or even newspaper could silence them for long. Always they wanted yet another change of book or newspaper, always they demanded. Let any nurse appear and a chorus of complaints would start up. Even then those nurses kept up a modicum of courtesy and patience.

But oh, the pity and the tragedy and the sadness of all such suffering – and the waste of time! Since none of those prematurely aged men, nor anyone else within those wards, need ever have got into such a state of ineptitude and decay. Nobody should feel so aged or become so mentally addled by pain and fretfulness, become so crippled, blinded, deaf or helpless. This was my profound reaction after several weeks in hospital, after watching scores of patients, after talking with them. This outburst may seem like plain nonsense to the sensible people who read it, who naturally accept pain and helplessness as a normal concomitant to old age. But who can deny that this would be a better and happier world to live in could it be freed from pain and helplessness – yes, and from old age as well?

Thoughts like this came because I had so seldom seen people giving way to illness, helplessly awaiting death, people so sorrowful. Yet after returning home, for some weeks I had to travel in an ambulance to and from hospital for treatment, usually picking up several other patients on the way. When talking with them I noticed how brave and enduring were the majority of these people, despite most of them having been treated for weeks and months with hardly any improvement, and often being faced with life-long disability. How brave and cheerful they were, and with what fortitude they accepted the prospect of a lonely and dependent old age. The tragic part was that I felt that the real cause of this hopelessness was within their inner selves, where neither hope nor promise glowed.

Confronted with this I came to feel how grievous it was that orthodox religion, once a comforting and sustaining factor in most people's lives, had been laid aside, forgotten; lacking religion these people had become chilled, empty and alone. Inevitably such inner emptiness and loneliness etch themselves permanently on face and form. Indeed, everything about a person either within the soul, or in the material life – his or her social status, trade or profession, prosperity or otherwise – duly imprints itself on the outer self during middle or later life. In youth these marks are superficial, in later life inescapable, and what writes itself most plainly is a feeling of emptiness within – that is, when the future seems emptied of any promise of good. Feelings tend to grow on us more readily than thoughts do and are more difficult to silence; they intermingle with the bodily self more readily, more noticeably.

On the credit side of my sojourn in hospital I recall what this experience taught me in the way of patience, and how to look at people's reactions to pain; their capacity to endure cheerfully, and often in an amazing and inspiring way, when everything looked grimly hopeless. Some must have known that little or nothing could be done for them, when illness or immobility had taken over so decisively. And yet their courage and cheerfulness endured.

Years ago I often used to walk along Kensington High Street, and finding the outlook rather unattractive usually took a kind of 'inlook' at various passers-by; by being watchful one can note the marks the inner man is making on the outer man, how it is affecting his gait, his bearing, even his habit of dress. So revealing were some of those faces in the High Street that they seemed to indicate even the kind of illness which would later develop.

Illnesses that should never happen. The time to tackle – and hopefully to cure – impending illness is while it is still lurking, and before it actually manifests in the body. Any such cure would have to consist of a change of thinking, an influx of warm, new feeling, brought about by a 'someone' taking a tender and compassionate interest in the sick person.

In this respect then, surely our National Health Service proves itself wrong footed when the emphasis is less on prevention than on cure. Treatment, it seems, too often begins near the sad finale, rather than at the good, bright and hopeful outset.

All this seems facile enough to write down but less easy to change, seeing that the real beginning of disease lies not in the body but in the mind and soul. Years ago, I myself looked upon the decrepitude of old age as something which everybody had to face up to sooner or later, and be conquered by; but later I began to feel, as I gazed on the suffering around me, that sickness and decay of the body was not in accord with spiritual law, not as God meant man to live; and that old age should be serene and healthy till the end.

Perhaps the wrong lies deep within ourselves. One half of our nature seems dolorous and inclines us to think and feel accordingly, whereas the other half attempts to raise us. We are subject continuously to the downward pull of the lower self, against the positive upward pull of the higher self, and it will be our long-persisting pulling down which lands us in hospital.

A cause of many complaints, of much inability in old age, is our habitual diet which from youth onwards consists of unbalanced, much processed foods far from the natural, whole and balanced food which is the ideal. Something like a thousand additives are mixed into our foodstuffs – colouring matter, flavours, preservatives, synthetic vitamins which mostly we consume without further thought. Yet the possibility is that even in minute quantities the long-term effect of such additives will be harmful. Nor are our foodstuffs in particularly good heart even before the chemist gets to work. Foods must be naturally, organically grown. Worst among our denatured, devitalised foods is bread, the staff of life, which is first robbed of its very substance, endowed with an unnatural whiteness, rendered wholly tasteless and then brought up to scratch by means of a hundred and one different additives.

Sugar is another sinner (or sinned against). In any case most of us eat much too much of it; the very way it grows – sparsely in sugar cane or sugar beet – shows that it was never designed to be eaten in concentrated form. Foods naturally grown, such as garden-produced vegetables and fruits, nuts, pulses, grains, if possible undoctored by chemist and manufacturer, will help us to a healthy old age free from disability.

One difficulty is that natural foods are not easy to obtain. Why should any citizen who knows better be obliged to eat denatured, devitalised, 'dragging down' foodstuffs because purer foods are unobtainable? Surely the greater the demand for wholesome foods the more plentiful should the supply become, and this indeed is already happening. Incidentally our fields would be more economically used by growing vegetable protein, instead of grazing animals destined for the butcher. It is estimated that eleven times as much food could be produced to the acre if land were used in this way. A well known health food doctor once told me that cancer cases among vegetarians are few and far between compared to incidents of the disease among meat eaters.

The strongest conviction I eventually brought away from hospital is that we must start right at the onset, when disease is brooding in a person's mind and emotions, afflicting his feelings and his disturbed soul, if a lasting cure is to be effected. Everything has to come out in time and will duly assert itself in the physical body. If you look at the faces of your fellow men you will find you can to some degree assess the manner of their thoughts, fears and frustrations – and maybe even their kind of illnesses, present or future. The suggestion that we need not wait for disease actually to arrive before it can be spotted may alarm. But it is possible, for potential trouble is threatening whenever one's line of thoughts and feelings gets too sore and painful; for example when we come to dislike heartily this or that happening, and would sometimes like to get our own back on someone or something; or when everything goes wrong because someone is getting a better deal than we are. Feelings such as these warn of illness starting up in the mind and soul, perhaps presently to sink down, but eventually to come out as bodily aches or pains. Sick thoughts tend to foster a sick body, while whole and wholesome thoughts foster a healthy body living a healthy life.

This is something medicine can do little about and the real attack on disease at its very source has to come primarily from ourselves. The difficulty is how to persuade ourselves that now, at this moment, is the right time, the obvious opportunity to tackle incipient illness. It is all too easy to make an excuse, think of a reason why now is not the time to change our thought patterns and living habits of many years. One such excuse could be, 'But how can all this be when babies are born with serious deformities or disease – obviously these aren't a result of their thoughts and way of life?'

In Maeterlinck's fairytale play 'The Bluebird', unborn children in the heaven world, destined to take on existence on earth, are shown preparing for their voyage down to their earthly mother, each one being equipped with various attributes likely to be useful during their new life. These include, note, the several illnesses they will suffer – brought over as a legacy from some past lives in order to teach the child (and maybe its parents also) something during its new span. Those who begin to think along these lines soon find they cease to seem fantastic and become acceptable. We are now beginning to think our way into a new awareness, asking ourselves whether many of our troubles and ills could be a continuation from some previous life, lived not too wisely, perhaps. The more one follows this line of thought the more logical it seems for it readily explains so many of life's problems, such as why one person seems to enjoy ease and plenty while another has a real devil of a time; why one enjoys good health (yet seems to live a very unhealthy life) and another vice versa.

If we can accept these ideas, we will the more easily see how and why some dire afflictions affect us and our fellows and why any treatment given has to treat more than just the physical symptoms. We have maybe to think years ahead of our time when doctors and healers will at last be looking for the cause of the sickness, not in the body but in the age-old soul.

This idea was put forward by Sir Arthur Conan Doyle in the

message he gave after his passing to the spirit world.* Sir Arthur outlines what medical practice might become in, say, fifty years' time. (And it should be remembered that he once practised as a doctor, so speaks from experience.) He says that medicine will deal not so much with man's bodily complaints as with the deep root cause of these ills, which lies in emotional stresses both in this and past lives and their effect on man's subtler bodies. (This presupposes, of course, the existence and availability of practitioners capable of coping with the deeper issues, and trained to look beyond the physical aspects – and this must surely come in time.)

He explains that a person's birth rays† may incline him towards this or that complaint. He groups disease under their respective four elements of Earth, Air, Fire and Water and suggests appropriate treatments:

The Earth Sign
The phlegmatic, the type liable to accumulate poison because of general sluggishness and lack of flow of vital force, can be grouped under this heading. There will be catarrhal conditions and subsequent poisons in the bloodstream, and other diseases which originate from such causes.

The Air Sign
Those under this group will often suffer from nervous diseases which act through the psychic centres. The head and back will be the most frequently affected.

The Fire Sign
Here there is likely to be emotional or mental trouble, inflammations and fevers. Treatment in such cases should be through the pituitary and pineal glands, and patients will respond readily to colour ray therapy.

* THE RETURN OF ARTHUR CONAN DOYLE published by the White Eagle Publishing Trust.
† The astrological signs under which the individual is born. Study of the birth chart can give a wise astrologer considerable insight into the soul's opportunities and limitations. In most charts all four elements are represented but usually one or two predominate.

The Water Sign
The Water Sign affects the lower part of the body, the legs and feet; being a fluidic sign those under it can be helped best by psychic or magnetic treatment.

Arthur Conan Doyle continues: 'If people would only follow these hints – and they are no more than hints – if they would use but a fraction of the application, experiment and research that is poured forth without stint on an inexact and speculative medical science, an exact and scientific method of universal healing would come about based on a real knowledge of man's physical, psychic and spiritual nature. If men really wished, their healing could become certain and precise in method.'

Already, then, we have a glimpse of what might be in the future; what we might call the happier way of healing. This will be one which starts long before sickness manifests in the physical body. Happier healing has to start in the thoughts, mind and whole attitude to life of every individual. What seemed so pitiful among the elderly patients around me in hospital was that most of their complaints looked like being permanent. They had come to an acceptance of permanent ill health. As I pictured their tense grey faces I could not help comparing them with the radiant, shining faces of the happy people I knew among the community in which I lived – people who had warmth and comfort radiating through their lives, who had lost fear of death, separation and loss, and who had sought healing in happier ways.

We do not have to drag wearily through life enduring sickness as best we can. After all, why should we saddle ourselves with pain or have our bodies cut about, leaving us but shadows of our former selves, when we could walk our ways in happiness, strength and usefulness to mankind? We should try to regard sickness, not as something to be endured, but rather as a challenge to be fought and overcome by a happier healing, a healthier outlook and a purer way of life.

Happier ways to prevent illness do not call for a great deal of time or money, but they do entail a more wholesome way of looking at life, a greater respect for all life. Effort is also required on the part of the patient; the will to fight any complaint mentally, knowing that the fault lies within no one but himself. The positive quality in the soul itself is that which can win through.

So the key to happier ways of healing lies beyond the physical body; it cannot be achieved by those who are completely imprisoned in flesh and deny the existence of anything apart from the material life. My friends are as they are because they have learnt beyond any doubt that the physical body and material life is but a small part of the whole self, the whole of creation, and their health and happiness stem from deep within. The purpose of this book is to show how you, how anyone, everyone, can leave forever the tense, grey and enduring band of sick, sad and suffering folk and join those who have found the happier healing.

2

THE HAPPIER HEALING

Rest quietly knowing that the wise Mother and the infinitely loving Father are bringing the children of the present age through sorrows, brought on them by over-indulgence in self will, into the sunlight of good will.

W.E.

This new edition of the book HEALING has been revised and partly rewritten mainly because of the recent hospital experience already described which brought home to me as never before the need for an approach to healing which would go much deeper than the treating of the physical symptoms.

Truly to be healed man must gain understanding of himself as primarily a spiritual being and accept this vital truth. This really means his acceptance of God as a working and transforming reality in his life. Once God becomes real to him then all else is seen in true perspective. In comparison, all other things become unreal or illusory. This includes illness in all its variations, for this also is unreal compared to the reality of God.

True it is that only great souls or those sorely tried and harrowed by suffering eventually reach this conviction. Once reached, then the Creator can heal His creature. This is a healing which by its very nature cannot fail to operate, a universal cure for disease in every one of its manifestations.

How can we even begin to define God? Some of us will doubtless stick to our childhood ideas of God as a superior being situated somewhere up above but reaching down to help people when they are up against it. My own idea is of an everlasting life force perpetually infusing all creation with its own vital essences which permeate every part of the visible universe, and the vaster invisible universes known only to more spiritual beings than ourselves. Life's great assertion of itself as indestructible and eternal – this, to me, best expresses God as an ever creative being. I believe God's life force floods every crevice of the ether – linking worlds together and holding the farthest universe within its grasp – omniscient, omnipresent.

The visible universe is infused by a spiritual essence without which nothing could exist. While still imprisoned in the physical life, the visible universe, one can see very little of the spiritual universe which interpenetrates it, and as yet we cannot know a fraction concerning that which awaits us; yet the promise of a land where everything is glowing, where God shines through and no ugliness creeps in, can reach or penetrate to us even here – and it is this glimpse and yearning coming from that luminous land which can give us healing.

Of all creatures living on earth man has the highest potential – not of course just in his physical body nor yet his mental, but in his spiritual quality. All creatures are within God's care and love. He sees potentialities where we see none; He sees man evolving capacities beyond our farthest dreams. He would have all men live as did Jesus Christ, and love as he did. God's interest and care is eternal – His interest in man's growth and evolution, the scrupulous care with which each detail of every creature's life is supervised. He would have man call upon His strength and power within to rise above the sickness of the physical and find true healing. Jesus demonstrated how the Christ (God) within can heal all ills, and Jesus said *He that believeth on me . . . the works that I do shall he do also.* So would God have all His children learn to do likewise – the potentiality is there, as is God's encouragement to keep on trying.

Some glimmering, therefore, of the reality of God and His loving care of each individual must be a first requisite of true healing. A person wholly imprisoned within his body, wholly relying on someone else for his healing, without effort on his part, might be a difficult case. True, results come even with the most obdurate, but this must largely be because a glimmer of spiritual realisation eventually enters; not until then does substantial and lasting healing start. When windows begin to open in the little darkened box in which most of us live, light enters in, and with the light comes healing. The more attuned the healer or patient becomes to God and His radiant life of spirit, the greater his range of healing or capacity to receive healing. Let no one feel deterred when doctors deny any chance of cure. Doctors do not always know. There is no limit to God's power nor to a patient's ability to receive when he opens the windows of his soul.

Having thought about God and the importance of belief in Him, if we are to achieve the happier healing let us consider how man's philosophy of life affects his body, mind and emotions, both when he is sick and even before the need for healing is realised. Disease is best dealt with during its infancy, not when it becomes a hardened old reprobate. In infancy, then, or even before – that is the real time to tackle disease. Small griefs or troubles, dislikes, angers or even hates, injustice, and other corroding irritants should be tackled or alleviated before they disturb the mind and feelings too deeply and thus become the root cause of subsequent disease.

Another basic cause of disease in human life is fear – our general uncertainty regarding the sundry bangs and blows which life brings or might bring. We feel that we live on the verge of a precipice of unknown troubles. The threat of what tomorrow, or for that matter the next hour or even the next minute, might bring, hangs over us so that we wobble along, riding on uncertainty, feeling that if only we knew exactly why we are here or whither we are going we could enjoy life. We try to believe that God is a Father of love, but how can we believe when we see so much suffering in the world? How can a God of love allow such things to happen? Then there is the fear of death itself. The worst aspect of the fear of death is probably the fear of being shut off from all that we call living – our own familiar, dear people and things. We may believe that man survives death, but we know little of the life hereafter and so fear the unknown, which apparently separates us from all we know and love.

Thus, more than just belief in the Eternal Spirit which permeates all life is needed to achieve the true and lasting healing, to achieve freedom from disease. A deeper knowledge of life, death and the hereafter, a greater understanding of the purpose of it all – a practical philosophy for everyday living, is needed. A philosophy such as this has been given to mankind at different times throughout the ages by many different spiritual teachers; it has become known by its students as the ancient wisdom. From time to time the same truths have been restated – the presentation may have been different but the truth within remains the same. Krishna, Buddha and Jesus were three such teachers, but there have been others. They come in succession to restate old truths in a new way, because the human mind tends to reject anything which it thinks old fashioned. It wants something new and different; and in any case the presentation of truth must suit the age in which it is given. The truths themselves, however, never vary; they are eternal and changeless. At this particular period of the world's history, there would seem to be a special and urgent need for such a restatement. On the one hand, new spiritual awareness, tenderness and humanity is abroad, perhaps awakened by the cruel harrowing man sustained during the two world wars. On the other hand we see multitudes of men expensively and with deadly purpose proposing to destroy their fellows and perhaps the earth itelf. The philosophy for living which follows has been given by White Eagle. Time alone will prove the value and importance of this restatement of the ancient wisdom, and certainly none can claim it to be the only truth, or indeed anything but plain and obvious truth relative to man's being.

White Eagle explains much about life on earth and in the hereafter, and this is the knowledge which can bring true and lasting peace to the soul, a peace which brings healing. Again and again he shows how all life is governed by divine law, and that there is no such thing as injustice or inequality. The truth of reincarnation, for example, explains a host of life's seeming inequalities. The law of cause and effect, or karma, explains yet more. This divine law ensures that each man reaps exactly what he has sown, either of good or ill. His reaping is not always at the physical level, for cause follows effect subtly and often within the soul rather than in the physical life. Men are but pupils in the school of life and lessons are sometimes hard for young and old alike, but those who come to recognise the law in operation will find it good, and realise that any pain endured proves ultimately beneficial.

White Eagle's teaching gives knowledge which can remove fear, knowledge which sustains in time of trouble, and knowledge which brings inner peace. He helps those who follow his way to glimpse the law in operation and so come to understand it and know that God is indeed a God of love; and the knowledge makes them happy. Should bereavement come their way, they know that death cannot separate them from those they love, and that communion and companionship between the two worlds is a reality. They know that the quality of their life in the next world will depend entirely on the quality of their life while on earth. They know the secret why and wherefore of their being. The bogey fear of death is removed and the dread of what might happen during mortal life dissolves away – thus ordinary people naturally become happier people who can not only receive true healing but also become healers themselves. Not all at once, of course; infiltration is the word, a gradual filling up of empty places in the soul. By reading the White Eagle books, by meditating on the thoughts they engender, peace of heart is gradually acquired. One has to fight, maybe, for it to stay there. Nothing worthwhile is easy of attainment; but the soul spiritually enriched becomes rich indeed.

It is now time for the writer to tell more of this teacher, White Eagle, and how his teachings came to be given and sent forth into the world in many books and recordings.

First who is White Eagle?* He is the spiritual teacher who uses my wife's physical body as the channel through which to speak. Those who know White Eagle revere his simplicity of spirit, his calm philosophy, his gentle wisdom and quiet humour, and accept him without question; while even those who have never heard his voice but read his books find his teachings inescapably true. The name White Eagle signifies a spiritual teacher and is not necessarily to be associated with only one incarnation. His usual

* See also the booklet WHO IS WHITE EAGLE? White Eagle Publishing Trust, New Lands, Liss, Hampshire.

personality is of an old American Indian chieftain, but he is also familiar to some of his friends as a Tibetan, an Egyptian Priest-Pharaoh, a humble brother in an obscure order, and an alchemist of the Middle Ages. Whatever bodies and personalities have been his in the past, he remains to us dear old White Eagle.

Now, what of White Eagle's medium, my wife, Grace Cooke – has she any extraordinary gifts or faculties which equip her for this work? Yes, indeed, I believe she has. From early childhood she displayed remarkable psychic and mediumistic gifts, the result, no doubt, of much training and work with White Eagle in past lives. (For example, we know they were together in South America when White Eagle was the wise Chief Hah-Wah-Tah and my wife his daughter Minesta.) In this present life my wife began her spiritual service in public in 1913, when she conducted her first Spiritualist meeting. In the years that followed she toured the United Kingdom giving proof of a life beyond death through her gifts of clairvoyance and clairaudience. White Eagle made himself known to her when she was still a child, but it was not until the late 1920's that he began to use her instrumentality, and started to give his beautiful teaching, his restatement of the ancient wisdom which has now made his name known and loved by so many. Eventually, he gave instructions that the time was right for a church to be formed solely for the White Eagle teaching and philosophy to be given to the world. Thus in 1936 the church, named the White Eagle Lodge, was opened at a small church hall in Kensington. (The name 'Lodge' was given as, to the Indians, a lodge is a place of refreshment, and this is what White Eagle said his church was to be for the many souls who would come in future years.) But before this happened some events took place which profoundly affected my wife and myself and the work which we have been called upon to do. In a remarkable way we were brought into touch and forever spiritually linked with the elder brethren of the ancient wisdom. The story which follows may seem strange and romantic and to some, perhaps, unbelievable, but it is true.*

* For the full and remarkable story, the reader should turn to THE RETURN OF ARTHUR CONAN DOYLE, White Eagle Publishing Trust, New Lands, Liss, Hampshire.

It all began early in the present century when a young French-
man, whose father was living in Rome, chanced to go on holiday
to Bagnaia, near Viterbo, about sixty miles north of Rome. Here
he met a hermit known as Father Julian, and an acquaintanceship
ripened into intimacy between him and the young man; at their
parting the hermit entrusted his friend with a manuscript yellow
with age containing the secret process of the Oracle of the Force
Astrale, a means of communication with masters of the Far East.
This the young man did not attempt to unravel until two years
later when, owing to great distress, he decided to consult the
Oracle.

The procedure involved the clear formation of a question,
which then had to be transposed into figures according to the code
given in the manuscript. The series of numbers thus produced
were subject to various processes and permutations. The answer
when it came was also in figures which had to be transposed into
letters and words to give a message wise and precise.

It was many years later that a message was received through this
means, instructing the young man to re-establish the group or
brotherhood of the Polaires, who would 'travel across the roads
of the world'. The purpose of the Polaires was to assist humanity
through certain 'years of fire' which were shortly coming to the
world (all this was happening in the uneasy period between the
two world wars), and to mitigate to some degree the forces of
hate and mistrust rampant in Europe before the advent of these
'years of fire'. The Polaire Brotherhood would work on the inner
plane of thought and feeling by using the unified thought power
(or better, soul power) projected by well trained groups working
for this purpose. The potential for good of such a concentration
of soul power could be incalculable.

Through the Force Astrale the Polaire Brotherhood learned
of Sir Arthur Conan Doyle's wish to transmit the knowledge he
had acquired since his passing in 1930. As the Oracle was too
tedious a method for such a long message, Sir Arthur told the
Polaires that his wife knew the medium to be used. When the
Polaires approached Lady Conan Doyle, she immediately con-
tacted my wife and a meeting was arranged with a messenger

from the Polaires. At this and subsequent meetings White Eagle gave proof of his close connection and work with the sages who were directing the Polaire Brotherhood. Subsequently Sir Arthur Conan Doyle used my wife to give his message (which is contained in the book THE RETURN OF ARTHUR CONAN DOYLE). We were both summoned to Paris to be initiated, in a secret spiritual ceremony, as brothers of the Polaire group, and were instructed to return to England and start a similar brotherhood group there. The English Polaire Brotherhood was started in an old manor house at Burstow in Surrey, where my wife and myself lived at the time. Gradually others were drawn to us and initiated into the work. The French group of Polaires dispersed, as far as we know, when Paris was occupied by the Nazis in 1940 and was not again reformed.

The English Polaire group later changed its name to the Star Brotherhood, dedicated to the healing both of nations and individuals as was the original Polaire Brotherhood. The Star Brotherhood became the nucleus of the White Eagle Lodge – and the outcome of its work for the individual sick is, of course, the happier healing set forth in this book.

Many messages had come through the sages before the French Polaire group was disbanded in 1940, giving further directions for the work of the Brotherhood. One aspect of their work was that of healing the sick by the same means of projected soul power. Some remarkable healing was accomplished by this means and, unlike the international work, its effectiveness could be demonstrated and proved. The international work by its very nature could not provide proof in the same way, but if the results of the work for individuals could be shown to be real and lasting why should not work with nations be equally effective? Angry and frightened governments were perhaps as sick in soul and in as sore a need of healing as were individual patients. Indeed, one cannot review the course of the Second World War without realising that something beyond material power saved the allied nations time and again.

Right from the start the Brotherhood has been the centre and focal point of all the work of the White Eagle Lodge. It has grown from the original two to a much larger group, all initiated by the leaders at a secret ceremony, as originally directed by the Polaire brothers; and as the inner work of the Brotherhood has continued and expanded since the early days, so too has the outer work of the White Eagle Lodge.

Not even the destruction of our premises in Kensington stopped the work. A new home was found and brothers and members were faithful and true; they attended meetings in London undeterred by darkened streets or air raids. Before the outbreak of war, groups had been formed to send absent healing to those in need and these, together with 'protection' groups, continued throughout the war with no sitter suffering injury, although one unfortunate person found his home wrecked on his return. (Perhaps his absence from home at the time saved his life.)

Shortly before the war ended White Eagle gave instructions that country premises were to be found; details were given as to where these were to be and in due course, New Lands, near Liss in Hampshire, was bought and turned into a place for spiritual retreat and study. New Lands subsequently became the administrative centre of the work, and the headquarters of the White Eagle Publishing Trust. More and more books containing White Eagle's teaching were published as the years went by. From the very beginning of the Lodge and Brotherhood work we have been supported by our two daughters and later their families. The work has always been run as a family concern, with my wife the mother not just of her small physical family but of the increasing number of members and followers of White Eagle. We must not think of her as someone living in an ivory tower but as one of the hardest workers in a practical sense too. Her enthusiasm and faith have carried the work through many difficult times. In her latter years she has been the inspiration behind the building of the White Temple on the hill top just adjacent to the New Lands gardens. Rome was not built in a day, nor yet the Temple, although it might almost be said that prayer has carried it along. Hard practical work steps in as well – but it is still prayer in essence which has brought an aura of blessing to New Lands, the Temple and its surroundings, and to which everyone responds.

This in itself brings a healing of the soul and spirit to those who come.

Nowadays not just two or three groups meet to send out absent healing as in the years of the war, but many many times this number. Each group is led by an initiated member of the Brotherhood, thus continuing the close link with the Polaires, and with the sages in the Himalayas and their powerful healing ray. As well as at the Temple and in London, groups meet also in many parts of Britain and the rest of the world. All follow the same method laid down by White Eagle; all put his teaching and philosophy into practice as a group and in their individual lives; and, by their study and their service, are learning to make the healing of the soul of man a living reality.

With this we leave our introductory words, and come now to the first of the many extracts from White Eagle's teachings that this book presents, chosen to warm, to comfort the reader; to go deep and stay long, not only in memory but in the heart, and so find expression in daily life.

3

THE CAUSE OF SICKNESS

*The elder brethren labour ceaselessly for you and for all men.
They do not judge their younger brethren because they know
God's laws, God's plan for the unfoldment of the God within
man. The young in soul are quick to pass judgment on
others; but the elder brethren are patient; they do not expect
too much.*

W.E.

White Eagle says: 'When we look upon humanity our point of
view differs somewhat from yours, because you concentrate as a
rule on the outer or bodily man whereas we see the inner man;
we see into his heart, we see his thoughts and motives, his feelings
and emotions. We can see beneath bodily ailments and behind
pain and suffering to their cause, and we try to help you.

'Broadly speaking, there is only one cause of sickness and this
cause is the lack of something within the soul of the man concerned, a state which prevents his receiving from the universal
spirit that man calls God.

'When we look into men's minds we see so much fear – fear of
discomfort or pain, fear of sickness, fear of poverty and indeed of
loss in any form; fear of loneliness and old age; and behind and
beyond all, often never faced or even admitted by him who fears
most, the fear of death.

'If, by some miracle, fear of death could be removed, this in
itself would go a long way towards healing all sickness. But this
cannot come about until man begins to unfold his spiritual self;
and then he attains a condition in which things formerly thought
unintelligible begin to grow clear and luminous, and death
becomes serene and beautiful, a mother come to succour weary
man in his last deep need.

'It is not so much the conscious as the subconscious mind of man that is ruled by fears, for the natural tendency of the conscious mind is to throw out such intruders as soon as possible; but once entertained by the conscious mind they root deeply into the subconscious, where each passing year establishes them the more firmly, so that they become a kind of shadowing background to the daily round, often darkening it with vague terrors and undefined anxieties. So many people fall into the habit of negative, unhelpful and depressing thoughts, and in the same way as lowered vitality lays its victim open to contagion, so also does a despondent mind invite accident or misfortune, the same law being operative in both cases.

'Train yourself therefore to look constantly above the dark things of life; train yourself to rise above your own enshadowed thoughts and depressed feelings, to think positively, hopefully. The good in life, all that is happy and constructive far outweighs the negative and destructive, so why invite trouble and ill health by dwelling on it? Think health, and in time you will become healthy. Real and lasting health can become a natural part of your being.

'Continually to know God is to know health, because as you learn to think God, to dwell upon the love of God, life within you grows more abundant, and disease has no place, no lodgement with you, for light casts out darkness.

'God is ever actively sustaining the good and bringing forth an ultimate and finer good from all evil. God is both personal and impersonal. Christ is for you the personification of the love of God; but do not confuse Christ, the Son, with Jesus the man, who came to demonstrate God by living among men as God would have every man live. Christ is the spirit which illumined the man Jesus with its flame; Christ is the Son, or the personal aspect of God which, dwelling in every soul, will endure, suffer and be crucified with that soul, if necessary, and bring to it an eventual resurrection.

'God is also impersonal in nature and in this aspect is the law which controls all nature on this earth and rules the stellar universes and the worlds of light to which the soul of man will some day migrate. Man cannot escape from this infinite and all-embracing law, and his well-being depends on his constant living in harmony with it; on his constant living in harmony with the constructive and the creative principle which rules God's universe. Jesus expressed this law quite simply when he said, *Love one another*, which means live in harmony, live calmly and placidly in the knowledge of God's loving wisdom which rules your life.

'God rules His universe by the law of love. You do not understand very much about the meaning of love, but you will; and through life's experiences you will learn how loving and wise is your Creator. Men cry out for God, and seek Him in many different ways. They look for Him in material things, but in the end all must learn that God is within them. God is in man's heart and in God, in man's heart, is all truth. When man turns within he will learn, through meditation and contemplation, the secrets of the universe. He will find God everywhere. He will see God in the stones, in the grass, in the flowers, the trees, in all growing things. He will find God in the oceans and in the rivers, in the valleys, on the mountain tops, in the heavens above the earth, the canopy of the stars. With inner vision he will behold and recognise the glory of God everywhere, and will be held in wonder at God's power and wisdom.

'But not only will man find God in these physical forms; he will also find God in his brother's heart. This will bring him the perfect happiness of heaven, for he will have become at one with all life.

'Truth must be realised in the heart. Book knowledge, intellectual pursuits will leave man ignorant of the deepest realities; only his own experience will teach him about God. The sorrows of life, the losses, the painful experiences which make him wonder if indeed there is a God – these are the things which will lead man eventually to find God within his own breast.

'If you have the will and the longing to find truth, to find God within you; if you aspire to that level of consciousness wherein you will know the meaning of God's love, and through your understanding are able to help others towards the light, then you will indeed see a golden harvest on this earth. Man creates as God creates. God has planted the creative power within man. Man is the child of God, and the spirit of God is in him. Man is composed of the physical body, the soul and the spirit. As man lives in spirit and by the spirit of God, so he will create a more perfect physical body, more harmonious surroundings, a life of beauty and perfection. This is a law, just, perfect and true.'

It would seem that man's first need is to get to know himself, that inner man of which he is barely conscious. White Eagle speaks of the fears which beset man, not so much in his conscious, as his subconscious mind. We should do well to consider what he means by those terms.

The subconscious mind should be thought of as an integral part of every human being, having being born with the babe. Perhaps it began to build the body of that babe from the moment of conception, who can say? But let us assume that with the birth of the baby, it immediately takes charge of its welfare. It directs and manipulates the internal arrangements of the child – its systems of ingestion, digestion and elimination, its breathing, its blood circulation, its very heart beat. It can prove itself very imperious, as every parent knows, when the baby feels hungry or uncomfortable. What it wants it will get, for it is a one-track mind, self-seeking and wholly egotistical in nature. It is this mind which renders the baby during its early years so self-centred a creature. Only later, when the conscious mind takes over to some extent, does a child begin to think of others and to show a degree of unselfishness.

It is both engineer in charge and unwearying worker for the body, having undertaken a lifetime job from the womb to the grave. This mind is our companion for every hour of the twenty-four hours of the day; we sleep with it and it wakes us, trudges along with us through our working hours, and is with us, still active, when we lie down to sleep at night. All the while it is pushing us along, keeping us going.

This part of our being is known by the occultist as the 'body elemental'; it directs the coursing blood, the breathing lungs, the beating heart, the digestion and elimination, and never in any adult sense grows up; it remains essentially childlike but by no means as innocent as a child – indeed, it was never innocent! For one thing it is in part an ancestral mind, for in it are stored the innumerable good and bad traits, qualities and idiosyncrasies which we inherit from faraway and forgotten ancestors, maybe saints and also many sinners who hang upon our ancestral tree. For all we know, our features, body, voice, gestures and colouring may be exact replicas of theirs. The subconscious then is an ancestral mind, the mind which secretes and yet hands on these things. It is also a mass or racial mind, because it is not separated as sharply as is man's conscious mind from the minds of his fellows, but on occasion takes its feelings from, or shares its emotions with, the mass mind.

Perhaps we should abandon the term subconscious in favour of the plainer term, the 'body mind'. Appertaining to the body as it does, it is concerned with everything that affects the body for good or ill. It registers everything happening within its domain, with an efficiency altogether denied to the conscious mind or intellect. With what precision do memories of early childhood forgotten for fifty, sixty, seventy years or more come welling back in extreme old age, when the conscious mind becomes enfeebled and the body mind takes charge again, as it did in infancy! This is indeed a second childhood, when the body mind, which was the body's original inhabitant, begins again to overrule everything else.

Not only are childhood memories infallibly registered, but all that happens during an entire life span – every thought and feeling – sinks down into the body mind and is there recorded. Furthermore, such memories become an actual part of the body mind, which in turn colours the head mind's outlook on life. So, if we store away a healthy outlook in our body mind, we keep ourselves healthy and happy. We can also reverse this simple process.

Here we come to the crux of the matter: what kind of thoughts about ourselves do we entertain habitually? Do we habitually instil thoughts of well-being into body mind – hourly, daily, month in, month out, year in and year out? If so, then we are surely conditioning it to healthy living. Or do we habitually think dolefully about our body? Does every ache and pain, every creak and crackle infect us with groaning apprehension? If so, then we are conditioning our body to a state of ill health. More important still, what is our habitual outlook on the world and our fellows? Is it kind, constructive, generous? Or is it critical, greedy, uncharitable? These thoughts and emotions will work on the body for good or ill. Constructive thoughts such as trust and love, faith, hope and charity can build health and well-being into the body; and on the other hand, negative, depressive thoughts, carking cares, as surely pull us down, saturating the body mind with fear, which later externalises itself. Watch a bird feeding and see the chronic nervous tension which grips it. It can so happen with the human body mind. Numerous are the varieties of fear available! Consider how the media exploit fear; how devotedly they dwell on disaster, accident and death.

Every thought of well-being or ill-being seeps down as feelings from the conscious mind to the body mind, and so the passing years gradually condition the body mind to manifest good or ill health, in strict accordance with the prevailing nature both of a man's daily outlook and introspection, and in accordance with the degree of fear implanted in it.

This habit of externalisation brings up yet another trait of the body mind – its love of dramatising itself. We can accept this because most of us in our conscious minds tend to do the same, so why shouldn't the body mind? Only when the latter takes the stage, as it were, does our head mind serve as an onlooker; and our body mind become the stage on which the actual performance takes place. Consider the common cold, for instance, for this is a long practised role that the body mind plays to perfection, from its disagreeable beginnings and onwards through the routine of sneezing, feverishness, coughing and spluttering. What possible reason can the body mind have for indulging in this sort of humiliating by-play? Because it has been gradually educated up to it by witnessing other innumerable body minds doing exactly the same thing. True, the head mind of the person concerned may take every precaution against catching cold; but when colds abound the lurking awareness of colds is stirring in the body mind, and this sets the stage and the performance takes place.

The Christian Scientist charges 'mortal mind' (which is another term for the body mind) with being the instigator of every form of bodily ill, and cures himself by steadily reconditioning mortal mind. By the end of this book we shall ourselves perhaps be in a better position to agree or disagree with this process. It is certain however that some people's mental attitude has indeed become so disciplined that they neither catch infectious diseases nor convey them to others, in spite of the fearsome array of germs and viruses which are said to abound. A doctor, as an example, can proceed daily from case to case, some infectious, some otherwise, and unless exhausted by overwork or personal troubles he will neither contract a complaint himself nor carry infection to any of his patients, and this in spite of his taking few precautions against infection – or so it would appear to the layman. The real safe-guard is, of course, the disciplined body mind of the doctor concerned – a mind kept in order by years of training, and obedient to the mass mind of medicine which has decided that doctors are immune from infection. The patient also has no apprehension in this respect, his body mind being conditioned not to fear infection from this source.

We have seen how faithfully the body mind can seize on any lurking fear in the conscious mind, and to the patient's surprise and dismay produce and dramatise a cold, more especially at seasons of the year when colds seem about due. Could this be because a kind of universal mind-infection precedes any infection by germs, because such thoughts are easily transmissible between body minds?

Could it be true also that the health and well-being of children is largely governed by the condition of the body minds of their parents? That is, by hopes or fears subconsciously entertained about those children by the parents. This applies especially to the mother. A mother whose childhood was spent, say, in an 'apprehensive' atmosphere, absorbs that atmosphere so that it becomes part of her mind and body and is apt to impregnate her home atmosphere with it. How then can the child do other than be affected?

We come now to the conscious mind – the waking mind, head mind or intellect; it is also called the frontal mind, and certainly it is always pushing itself in front – a detail perhaps symptomatic of self-importance – as compared with the seemingly unobtrusive body mind. It is the instrument with which a person copes with everyday life and problems, the interpreter (and to some extent the *limited* interpreter) of the things registered by the five senses of man. None can deny that man's intellect, reasoning power and invention have brought him far. Nevertheless it has its limitations, tending to crystallise truth and side with the letter which killeth rather than the spirit which giveth life. Intellect is not necessarily intelligence. Against the claims of the body mind it is rather frail; indeed, we must ask ourselves whether the head mind can ever subdue and overcome the sturdy resistance of the body mind, even by its utmost efforts. The answer is almost never; although there are cases where sheer will power has triumphed over some tragic affliction. Even then that head mind has probably been reinforced by something far more vital – in fact, by the strongest resource, the most potent ally, on which man can call in his deep need: the mind in the heart.

If you analyse the headlines in your daily paper you will see that this is mostly a head mind world, a head-directed world, wherein intellect calls itself intelligence and worldly sense counts for more than spiritual wisdom. Man's deeper intelligence, how-ever, and his seat of wisdom is not found in his everyday, head mind. Here is the case for the mind in the heart.

4

THE MIND IN THE HEART

Deep within your heart is a never-ending spring of life and power; as you can live within this life and light, you will become a brother of the light, and cannot fail in your efforts to help mankind.

So be courageous and be true to the Christ light within you. Let the light flow through your being, so that the healing touch and the healing word is yours. Thus will the whole of the earth be raised.

W.E.

Most people remain ignorant of the existence of this mind in the heart – yet not altogether ignorant; for few traverse a whole life span without some promptings from this higher mind, without some quickening of an inarticulate and yearning sense of beauty, some vague spiritual stirrings and strivings, some glimpse of a divine power and justice overriding the chaos and the injustice of the material world. Deep within us a spiritual consciousness functions; deep within us we feel – not with the shallow, temporal and sometimes frantic turmoil of the emotions – but strongly, richly, ineffaceably.

On occasion this profounder consciousness takes charge of us, when for instance we are faced with special danger or an acute emergency, with catastrophe or despair, and when, to our own amazement, by some miracle of strength or of patience, courage and steadfastness, we have won through. This has happened because some deeper self than the ordinary daily self of mind and body has taken over, and we have obeyed its injunctions.

It can happen on a national scale; we have only to look back to those years which preceded, and anticipated the Second World War and made it inevitable, and remember how Britain was slothful, heedless and careless to a degree. Some thought she would never again rise to meet the challenge. During that period Britain was heedless of her spiritual heritage, of her record of world service and leadership, of her responsibility to the world. This was a Britain deeply in the grip of body mind, and therefore immersed in those things thought essential for bodily welfare – a nation material in mind and outlook. When war came (which itself most surely originates from the body and head minds of man) what a change took place! What took charge to effect that change? None other than the awakening heart mind of the nation. Now let us try to define that heart mind.

We must go far back here. None knows the true story of this land or of her people. We must go back beyond the age of the barrows which house the dead on the chalk downs of Britain, beyond the mighty cromlechs and circles of standing stones. Avebury and Stonehenge are of recent origin in comparison with the times and peoples we are seeking.

We must go back to a time when this land was warm and sunlit, with a genial climate; when it was peopled with men and women new on the earth (for the human race did not evolve from any ape-like animal). In the beginning man was a spiritual being emanating from the mind of God. Wholly pure and innocent of experience of good and ill alike, man set out on a journey which was to prove him to the uttermost. In the course of that journey he descended into a world of matter. He took upon himself the coat of skin mentioned in Genesis, meaning the body of flesh. Before that stage he had inhabited an etheric body – this was his Eden period, also told about in Genesis. Later, by reason of his fleshly body, he was shut out from Eden (or his etheric world), and became a tiller of the soil, a dweller in a wilderness filled with weeds. That wilderness symbolised his new human nature, and the weeds his failings. Presently, so low did he sink that his higher self was slain by his lower; in other words, Cain slew Abel. Afterwards the punishment of Cain was greater than he could bear. It has been so ever since and with it grows the urge which eventually leads man back to God.

So we are back at man's beginning, with the race of men wandering in their own wilderness. Man could not be left in such a condition for ever. He needed help, guidance, comfort. So teachers came to succour men. Where did they come from? Mostly, it would seem, from other and more advanced planets than the earth. They voyaged, those great and wise ones, from more beautiful worlds than this, the darkest planet. They were, it is said, wondrous to look upon, with grace and beauty far exceeding that of men. They were masters of themselves and therefore masters of their environment of matter. Even the very stones obeyed their command. This is how stone temples of a size and majesty which stagger our present-day imagination came into being. In an infinitely distant past, vast buildings or temples were constructed by use of a power exceeding that of mortals.

The dwellers in the wilderness were taught by these wise ones; divine truth was imparted to them concerning themselves, their souls, their destiny; and about invisible spiritual worlds existing beyond the physical state. Some became sanctified, powerful of spirit. Even at his lowest, man has never been altogether divorced from his etheric life though it has become overlaid by physical life and matter. Yet every man leaves his imprint on the etheric world around him with all that he does and is; so does he on the physical, but not to the same extent. Transient physical matter is always changing; but what etheric matter registers seems to remain for all time. Thus the life, thought and action of every man leaves its stamp on that matter more or less for ever.

A visit to various battlefields, or to slaughter-houses where masses of animals are killed, or to places where hideous crimes have formerly been committed, will confirm that a dark stain of sin and horror has been registered, not so much on the physical, but on the invisible etheric world of the vicinity.

It can be reasonably argued that if an evil deed (or an evil life) leaves so dark a stain on the etheric, so also will a good, a sainted life leave a corresponding bright mark or radiance. And, further-more, that any such radiance left behind will be even more lasting than an evil stain because, broadly speaking, evil has a natural tendency eventually to destroy itself, by its very nature.

Let us recall some examples of places where good lives have left their radiance. Twenty miles from where these words are written is Winchester Cathedral, a majestic building standing on the site of a far older holy place. From this site and from the building itself radiations pour forth across the downlands which surround the city. Some people are sensitive and feel them, others are insensitive and ignore them. Nevertheless, they are as real as the sunlight, and can illumine the souls of men.

It is the same with the hill temples which abound in this land. Some, such as Stonehenge and Avebury, attract many visitors. If you visit them try to go alone. Go prayerfully, ready to worship. Climb the chalk downs, crisp turf beneath your feet, with the lark overhead singing its praises to its Creator. Take example from the lark. Lives have been spent here dedicated to God and man – holy lives, lives that have been laid down in service. *Greater love hath no man than this, that a man lay down his life for his friends.* Such men and women have lived and died on these hillsides, and their bodies are now one with the bright chalk soil. It is from the record such lives leave on the ether that the radiance comes and always will.

Feel the power, feel the purity, of these hills of Britain. Here is her heart – the mind in the heart of Britain. Custody of that heart can be given to no church, to no government, to no body of men, and none can ravish it. The broad hills enshrine it, the larks sing its praise, and the bright sky and mounting clouds are its temple and its sanctuary. Men ignore these things, even jeer at them. But when the emergency arises, when the challenge comes and Britain herself is imperilled, what happens? The heart of Britain takes charge and, with a nation as with an individual, the new man stands revealed. Hitherto, he has been only a man with body and head minds – two-thirds of a man; now the heart self and the heart mind complete him, and he confronts his foe. This man and the spirit in him is such that none can gainsay him. Patient, tenacious, steadfast, good humoured, he manifests the true qualities of his race. Whence come these qualities? They are part of his soul because they are also charged with the very substance of Britain. They emanate from her soil and air, sea and sky, and most of all they are the heritage won for Britain by sainted and heroic lives. They are her shield, her true defence. None shall penetrate them; none could penetrate. Men affirm that this or that lucky chance saved Britain; that chance has always saved her despite her unreadiness and desperate need. Britain was saved not by chance but by design, and to serve an ultimate end which will some day make all her sacrifice worthwhile.

We have told of the mind in the heart of one nation in order to illustrate our meaning. But what of the mind in the heart of the individual? How shall this be defined?

The individual man, generally speaking, is in much the same condition as was his nation during the so-called years of peace between wars, with only two-thirds of him functioning body and head minds – and inadequately equipped for living, because the creature is in part separated from its Creator. This Creator, Whom we call God, never Himself cuts off man from his source of spiritual supply. On the contrary, the two are linked together more intimately than man can believe possible. Each man is an idea held in the mind of God. So also are the whole world, and the universe which is its frame, God's thoughts made manifest. Were any man to be forgotten by God for any fraction of a second, that man would be annihilated. Yet man himself can forget God and in his forgetfulness seemingly cut himself off from God. In spite of this, man seems to be as necessary to God as God to man. The Kingdom of God can only evolve as man himself evolves, and a hold-up on man's part means a hold-up for God. We have to put out of our minds for evermore the idea of a God Who requires constant placating, Who is full of whims and partiality for any nation or any church. What we have wonderingly to believe in, trustfully and lovingly to accept, is the idea of a God Who seeks man's love, Who wants to be loved and trusted, Who wants to companion man until God and man merge into one, and man lives ever cherished by the divine kindness and mercy. Such a conception as this, White Eagle tells us, contains the essence of the revelation of Jesus Christ to mankind. The Father of Whom Jesus spoke was Father to every living soul of man, so closely present with man that He suffered every pain with man. This is what Jesus affirmed with his words, with his miracles, and with his life itself.

Can we believe this essential truth about God and man? Why should we believe? Only because something within us tells us that it is true; somewhere, deep within, we have the power to recognise truth. By this power we shall presently understand that the whole of life, with its every trouble, perplexity, problem and difficulty – not to speak of its pleasures and joy – is designed for no other purpose than to bring about an awakening in us.

Where is the power to recognise truth sited in man, and in what part of him does he feel truth? In the etheric heart, or the mind in the heart, situated in the centre of the breast. Through this mind man is linked to God, because it is the Christ in him. Such a link may function strongly and efficiently: in that case there comes a constant inflow of life force from God to man. Or it may be weak and failing: in which case the person languishes for spiritual light and air and drags along through life.

Whatever his circumstance sooner or later man must consciously draw near to God, for God is his very life. Once this happens his wanderings in the wilderness will cease; he will become complete, balanced, capable of harmonious living and of maintaining a happiness the world can never take away. He will become healed and whole, and is in a fair way to becoming a victor in the battle of life.

Let us settle what is meant when it is said that the mind in the heart is Christ in the heart. What then is Christ? Here White Eagle must speak:

'Jesus, we are told, was thirty years of age when he started his ministry; that is, when the dove, or the Holy Spirit descended on him after his baptism at the hands of John. This tells us that Jesus, as a master, had by then been made ready to receive illumination, or the great initiation, when his body, mind and soul surrendered to the Christ spirit, and became the prepared, perfected and purified instrument for the supreme manifestation of the Christ light and power. So great a power as this could not be contained in the body or soul of a child or youth, or in an ordinary man, but had to wait during years of preparation until the human channel was made ready.

'So we have two distinct yet interpenetrating stories to consider; one telling of Jesus of Nazareth, born in the brotherhood of the Essenes, of selected and consecrated parents; the second telling of the manifestation through Jesus of the Christ spirit, or perfect Son of God, only made possible by his age-long preparation and selfless sacrifice. This is the mystery interpenetrating the simple Christian story of the birth, life and death of Jesus.

'Some think the biblical records of the life and death of Jesus of Nazareth are inaccurate; and the most they will believe is that some minor prophet called Jesus or Joshua once lived and later died a natural death in Judaea. We, of our inner knowledge, testify that Jesus was born the son of a craftsman in the brotherhood of the Essenes, and that the story of the crucifixion, understood mystically, is a true story of the Christ spirit; but intuitive wisdom from the centre of truth is needed in order to understand its true meaning.

'We say also that Jesus the Master still lives and still answers the prayers of his people; that Jesus the Master is still behind the work of all true Christians, whether orthodox or unorthodox. For it is true that after the drama of the crucifixion was complete – a drama so great and wonderful that all men will some day bow down in wonder and praise – Jesus lived on. The crucified body was endowed again with life (or its purified particles resuscitated) and he withdrew into the secret places of the mountains, to live in one of the mystical centres which then existed in Syria. Can he still be seen by the faithful? Yes, his presence form comes; he stands beside the communion altar; he still has power to heal the sick, to comfort the mourner, to bless and sustain men in their need. But Christ, the Son of God, is not the man Jesus; Christ is the universal spirit, the way, the truth and the life, the Grand Master of all the mysteries.

'Do not confuse Jesus, the man, with the Christ, the Son. Although in the gospels the two seem blended and as one, nevertheless a clear conception of the qualities of each is essential. The Christ spirit is the power which has been since the beginning. *As it was in the beginning, is now, and ever shall be. . . .* The voice that spoke through Jesus affirmed: *Before Abraham was, I am,* thus indicating that the Christ was older far, was indeed timeless and universal spirit, as compared to the man of earth. Christ had his being in the heart of God even before the beginning of the world. Therefore let us accept Christ as the Son of God, and believe that this Son manifested through Jesus, the Master of the Christian mysteries; and let us believe that Jesus was so conceived, born and trained, that he might provide a channel for the manifestation, or expression in mortal life of Christ.

'God resides in the heart of man in the form of His Son, the light, the love of Christ. The Son of God is the light, and is the life of all earthly creatures. *In the beginning was the Word, and the Word was with God, and the Word was God . . . And God said, let there be light. . . .* The light was the first-born of the Father-Mother God, and the light shone in the darkness, in matter, in earth, but the darkness comprehended it not.

'In the physical sense, the light of the sun illumines your life and enables you to see all kinds of beautiful form on the earth; if the light was not there, and you were in a state of darkness, you would be unable to see any beauty on earth. Moreover you would have no food to sustain you, because the sun gives the food which feeds the physical life.

'The physical sun also has a spiritual aspect, a spiritual body, and by the light of the spiritual sun you perceive truth, you see God. You have a physical body; but you also have a spiritual body and a divine spirit which is the illuminator of your soul. And when your soul is developed spiritually, your physical body too is illumined by this same divine spirit.

'What has all this to do with the chaos and suffering on the physical plane, you ask? It has everything to do with society, with human life on earth; because when the divine spirit, the spark of life in man, the Son of God, is able to find full expression through the human character and the human soul, it will transform the whole of life.

'You will say, "But when man gets to that state of evolution he will not be living on the physical plane at all, he will be in the spirit world." Well, we in spirit would not make such a statement. All we know from our teachers in the halls of wisdom is that man is a babe, a child living on the earth; and God has endowed that child with the power to master the physical state of life. In His love and wisdom God has embodied the spirit and the soul in physical matter in order to give that individual spirit the opportunity of evolving into the perfect man.

'Christians think of the Perfect One, the Son of God, as Jesus – Jesus, the great initiate who had so perfected himself in body, mind and soul, that he was able to be a channel for this Great White Light, this love, this Son of the Creator, which is and always has been and ever shall be the salvation of humanity. But we know that in the degree that this light can manifest through man so will the whole of mankind save itself. Every man can become a christed one, a saviour. Your Christian faith tells you that the Son of God, Jesus Christ, will save you. But we are telling you from the world of spirit that this divine light, the divine love, the first-born of the Father, is in man himself; and so man himself, through the Christ in him, is his own saviour.

'What says this voice of Christ within the heart? How can we find words to tell truly of that voice which some people ignore and some never wake to hear? It comes as a whisper from the innermost, perhaps never more than a dim yearning, a hunger for something that transcends and surpasses bodily joys and achievement, a reaching out for that which can resolve all discords, transmute all fear, a hunger which nothing of the earth, of a physical nature, can satisfy. To some people life seems to bring little but disillusion, disappointment, suffering and heartbreak; they teach their own lesson; for some the path lies through joy and thankfulness, which lift the responding soul closer to God. These experiences are part of the path which, soon or late, all must traverse in their search for Christ.

'The voice of Christ within the heart of man is the voice of kindness, teaching forbearance, holding no taint of harshness or criticism. Who indeed dare criticise when each soul follows its self-appointed path? It teaches humility of thought and spirit. "Not I . . . but only the transcending power of God, which knows me better than I can ever know myself, and can perfect me despite my many frailties – that and that alone doeth the works." '

It will be clear by now that this book does not so much suggest a cure for this or that disease, but will outline a way of life which has power to heal. To this end we have briefly described the body mind and its functions, and touched on the powers and limitations of the head mind when it is divorced from the mind in the heart. The biggest shortcoming of the purely head mind is its inability to apprehend spiritual truth. Confronted with reasons for faith in the existence of God or the reality of Christ as a personal and ever-present influence; with the evidence of the continuance of human life beyond death; with the case for reincarnation, or for the law of karma (karma means that effects inevitably follow causes in every department of human life), it is out of its depth. *Of itself* it simply cannot apprehend or comprehend the significance of these mysteries. This is not to condemn that mind. The head mind has its own particular function, as has the body mind, which it fulfils with bewildering success; but we shall function only as two-dimensional beings so long as we are ruled by the body and head minds alone. We have been designed to become three-dimensional beings comprising body, mind and spirit. We are made in the image of God, spiritually, and can also become so bodily or mentally to some degree, according to our physical and mental health and wholeness. As twofold beings we can never attain to our full stature or completion or full harmony of life.

Broadly speaking, man lives as a bodily being during his first years; as a head-mind, reasoning creature during early manhood and onwards into early middle age; but all the time he should be developing a degree of spiritual intelligence and comprehension of the whence, why and whither of his own being. This done, life will become more reasonable for this pilgrim of eternity.

Most of us when taking a journey, make preparations for it.

The one journey that seems inescapable for Everyman lies through death of the physical body to the life beyond. Oddly enough, people see no necessity to prepare for this, chiefly because they are frightened, their development having stopped short at the head mind. This fear is the cause of most of the inharmony and sickness which beset us.

Go into any street in any town in any country, and with a new insight study the faces of the passers-by. On how many of those faces will you see serenity, peace, happiness, or that bloom and look of permanence which comes from a tranquil heart and life? How many faces, on the other hand, will you find criss-crossed by pain, and lined and harrowed by the years? Leave the youthful faces out of your investigation, since body and head minds content youth. The testing time comes in later middle age, when materiality palls, and the bright thread of life grows thin – the thread that links the creature to the Creator. But should the link grow stronger instead of weaker with the passing years, the creature will know increasing fullness of being.

All this is not to argue the point about anything, or try to persuade anyone to adopt this or that outlook. It is only to state facts no thoughtful person can deny. Perhaps it is not wholly the *reason* of man which shies away from truth, but something even stronger – his innate reluctance to make a spiritual effort. Perhaps the good Lord has extra patience with us because He sees that sloth and stupidity and not black sin are really our arch-enemies! Be that as it may, something considerable has to be overcome in the sufferer whose fixed belief is that he has only to pay money to someone to be helped back to health, and thereafter need make no further effort. This unfortunately applies to healing both orthodox and unorthodox. Even in spiritual healing the patient is apt to expect Providence to do everything, while he himself merely sits and waits to be healed. This cannot be the true way to heal or to redeem the self. We are therefore seeking something which rings true, which is satisfying and valid by its very nature. White Eagle has a wise heart – surely and tenderly he will guide us into this way of truth.

5

GROWTH INTO WISDOM

The temple from which Jesus drove the money changers is man's own body. You are that temple, and within you dwells the spirit of God. But if you submit to the lower nature that is greedy, self-centred and fearful, you will fill your temple with thieves and robbers. Then the Christ, or the Master within you, will rise up and say, 'Begone! This is the house of God!'

The perfect plan

White Eagle says: 'A divine and perfect plan exists for the development of man's soul; when your vision opens you will begin to understand something of the wonder and magnitude of that plan.

'Some people concern themselves far too much with what they call evil and darkness, until mentally they are continually combating these forces. From one point of view they are right of course. To you on earth evil seems a very active and opposing force. It *is* an opposing force, but we must remember that opposition has its place, much as have the natural elements of force and energy; for if force were not resisting the energy in nature something cataclysmic would follow. You must try to look upon these two conditions – evil and good – good and evil – as two great opposing elements which maintain the world on its course, the one being complementary to the other. We may liken the two to centrifugal and centripetal force, since the one is *driving out* and the other is the *turning in*, or the *driving in*. The evil appears to be that which is driving *in*, and so we liken this force to selfishness; such great human selfishness tends to draw everything to itself, while unselfishness, love, projects, radiates light, and is the *re-creating* element. It is necessary to view dispassionately in this way these two aspects of good and evil as forces or elements which are both necessary in human life.

'If you are patient and meditative, you will find that what appears to be evil always has a way of bringing forth eventual good. Indeed, good comes out of evil, and evil has its part to play both in the evolution of humanity, and in the evolution of life itself.

'If man really understood the spiritual laws which rule his own life and that of all creation he could never again sin, never wilfully violate those laws. It is because man does not understand the spiritual law of love that he sins. Once he has gained fuller understanding he can never again sin, he will do no evil.

'Men seek for knowledge, but no amount of factual knowledge will confer the wisdom which brings understanding of spiritual law. Wisdom is a quality of the soul whereas knowledge is mostly of the intellect. Seek then for true spiritual knowledge; seek the wisdom of the spirit, of the Christ within. If you will seek your contact with God earnestly and continually through prayer and meditation, understanding and wisdom will come to you, you will find that you can even tap into universal knowledge, that deep wisdom of the heavens and the heart wherein truth abides. Whatsoever your spirit needs to know, that knowledge it can acquire, for it is there, in your heart.'

Proving God for yourself
'Many of you must have proved this in your own way. You have prayed for guidance or help in some problem and it has come, although probably not as you were expecting; it has come in God's way, not yours. So always turn to God in your need; go to God as you would to a loving parent. *But seek ye first the kingdom of God, and his righteousness; and all these things shall be added unto you.* It comes down to this plain fact: that you must learn to become humble, simple and confident in God.

'The fundamental cause of all the manifold diseases of men is a lack of spiritual light in the life of man; and the one true cure is the incoming of the light of God into his life. Within your heart is what we will call the permanent life cell; and from this per-

manent life cell your whole being can be recharged or recreated.
Whenever you truly aspire to God and make your contact with
the Lord Christ you are receiving his light and life force into this
life cell, and this, through your own heart mind, can gradually
recreate, rejuvenate and renew your body. This is the way to true
and perfect healing as demonstrated by Jesus, the secret of eternal
youth and life. Jesus was the greatest demonstrator of this divine
power. Jesus did not concern himself with the names of diseases.
He always went to the spiritual cause. He healed by pouring
in the light, pouring in the spiritual rays which awaken the
soul.'

Spiritual law in the material world
'Throughout his life Jesus taught and demonstrated the spiritual
law which governs all life. His parables describe the law again
and again; his miracles demonstrate it – how the spiritual law
works in a material world – above all, the law of cause and effect.
From within the veil we too are able to see the working of this
spiritual law in the material world. We see, for instance, how
thoughts of love and good will create good, create peace and
happiness, create beauty. On the other hand we see how resentment, selfishness, greed and hatred create chaos, unhappiness and
ugliness.

'Do you realise that when man gives way to these lowest
emotions he becomes controlled by the body elemental,★ or
lowest self, and the higher self, the angel, is driven out? Man is so
inclined to be overruled by the body elemental, which is always
only too ready to take possession. When Jesus cast out evil spirits,
these were not necessarily other human entities. The obsessed
sufferer can just as likely be in the grip of this lower elemental,
which has obtained domination over him. Do you see how Jesus
demonstrated the spiritual law when he cast out devils and healed
the sick? He was demonstrating the power of Christ in man to
overcome the weakness of the lower self, and make man perfect.
When he was putting forth the power of the Father, he was
reaching to the patient's higher self, calling it into operation,

★ Akin to body mind, cf. chapter 3.

giving it power to assert itself and take possession of the sick body, thus driving out all that was inharmonious. When he raised the dead, he called upon the spirit; he gave power and life to that soul, enabling it to return and take up its work again on earth.

'Some would ask whether Jesus was not thus interfering with the karma or with the free will of the patient. We would have you remember that the Christ within you can transmute your karma. We emphasise the power over physical matter of the Christ spirit in man. With most the lower self is in control; but when the higher self reaches out and receives the power of Christ there is nothing it cannot accomplish. Christ then changes darkness into light and disease into perfect harmony.

'The greatest obstacle to this Christ healing is the self below the daily consciousness – the subconscious self. As soon as that can be illumined by the inflow of the Christ power through the highest self, then the life is enriched, the body healed. The negative thoughts that are part and parcel of the lower self are real and have power, not only over the ordinary, conscious life, but also over the subconscious life – which plays havoc with man's health and happiness. But when the soul fully realises his kinship, his at-one-ment with the divine life and allies himself with the Christ, then he is healed, made perfect.

'No power on earth can touch the man illumined by the divine life, and the Christ love shines forth from him to heal and bless mankind.

'Practise those truths which Christ came to teach. . . . *And thou shalt love the Lord thy God with all thy heart, and with all thy soul, and with all thy mind, and with all thy strength. . . . Thou shalt love thy neighbour as thyself.* Positive laws; positive injunctions upon which hang all the law and the prophets! There can be no compromise. Endeavour in humility and simplicity to put into operation spiritual law in the material world. The body elemental makes man lazy, and he finds it easier to go the way of the world. But you must learn to recognise and deny the claims of the lower self and of the body elemental, and to the best of your ability attune yourself to the divine self, divine love. Then witness the effect on your body, on your life. But let your effort be not for yourself but for the common good. Do right for right's sake and because the love of Christ constrains you to desire only one thing – to help your brother, not by interfering with him, but by giving him good will and kindness, understanding and gentleness. Thus you will become a son of peace, a true child of God.

'Disease has become so generally accepted as a part of life, and medicine has bestowed so many interesting names upon it that it is difficult for you to accept what we say; nevertheless we re-affirm that all disease springs from one cause, an inner spiritual origin that has its final outworking in the physical body.

'Beyond the head mind lies the heart mind or the spirit of man, and you must go further than the body to find the real origin of disease. Let us take a very simple example; we would not hurt or offend anyone, but is it not strange how often people who feel sorry for themselves because of the heavy burdens with which (as they think) Providence has saddled them, suffer from troubles in the back? Others feel pains in their feet and legs; do these perhaps arise because they lack courage to step forward with confidence in God? So we associate leg and feet trouble with lack of faith.

'There are also those who refuse to recognise or admit spiritual truth, or who refuse to listen to the voice of the spirit when it speaks to them. We are inclined to associate eye or ear trouble with such refusals, which are not necessarily of this life, or the conscious mind. These things lie so deeply within the soul that very often the head mind has no knowledge of them.

'We give you these ideas to show you how important to health it is to shed your troubles and your fears of some impending and dreadful complaint, for while it is imprisoned by fear the mind cannot see truth; when you are fearful about yourselves you are doubting God's power.

'Now, truth is very simple; it is also profound with a pro-fundity beyond the reach of intellect. He who would find this truth within himself must first become simple, as a child is simple in its affection and belief, simple in its response to kindliness, in its love for life. All beauty, love and kindliness are essentially true; and it is also true that having yourself become simple you will

begin to understand profound truths which cannot be glimpsed or
grasped without this simplicity of heart.

'Fear is the great enemy of any such realisation of truth. You
must begin to change this condition; you must refuse to believe
that negative things are as real as they seem. Only man by his
attitude and reaction lends to them a sort of reality. Train yourself
to look habitually into the light of God. See Christ within your
heart encompassing the world by his love. Learn never to entertain or talk about depressing things, never to wallow in symptoms
of disease or descriptions of pain and suffering, because all the
while your subconscious will be listening, taking it all in, only to
reproduce it in some form on your own self. Remember always
that what appears as threatening, painful and destructive to the
outer self, must by its very nature be something transient.
Negative things disperse and destroy themselves simply because
they must. . . .'

Fighting back against sickness
'Maybe you are at the moment sick? Try to realise that this
sickness is something you are steadily building up within your
two minds by nourishing fear of it. Refuse to accept what is being
so insidiously suggested. But of course you must remember also
that you cannot ride roughshod over what are called 'natural
laws'. That is to say, while you are young in spiritual truth you
must to a degree defer to preconceived opinions and not refuse to
seek the aid of medical science if this be thought necessary. Do the
wise and right things with all your problems of health or sickness
in these early stages. Later, as you learn to live more calmly and
placidly, you will be able to resist, and rise above these problems
by the power of Christ in you.

'In the degree that you learn to live more wisely and peacefully,
so will your health improve and dreaded complaints vanish. Some
of you are perhaps too fond of running to doctors at the slightest
pain, or of relying too much on material aids. The divine light and
the divine companionship will rid you of all aches and pains, if you
will only pay the price in service and constancy.

'Concentrate on right thought. This right thought should be

God thought throughout, pervading the whole being. Meditate on this tremendous truth and you will see its significance. Right thought is essentially balanced, loving and kind, tolerant and generous. Right thought means a good outlook on life, always.'

6

ARRESTINGLY NEW AND STRANGELY SIMPLE

The elder brethren live to serve God and man. They work continuously, meditating and strengthening their consciousness of God, and sending to humanity the light and power which radiates from them as a Brotherhood. They would have you know that you may receive the strength of their love. Whatever you need, whether it be in sickness, loneliness or anxiety, look towards them and you will receive immediate help, power and peace, and a sense of well-being.

A new world is shining behind the veil. Do not doubt; do not fear; live continually in the company of the shining ones, the companions of the spirit. Do not be misled by so called commonsense and reason. They have their place and give you balance, but do not be blinded by them. Look beyond, to the true life of God.

W.E.

We have tried to seek out the cause of all disease, and not of any one disease in particular, together with the causes behind those ill-defined hungers or neuroses, such as the chronic weariness, boredom, depression and hopelessness which afflicts so many lives.

White Eagle tells us quite simply that disease comes about through lack of spiritual light in man's make-up. Can anyone deny that something is missing from the make-up of the average man or woman, and could that missing element be the light – spiritual illumination as White Eagle says? Can it be that we are meant to develop that light, that spirit, as an essential part of our normal equipment for life, and that without it our lives are impoverished?

With this in mind, consider the normal development of a human being, the unfoldment of mind and character expected of him during his life span. His infancy and childhood are devoted, as we all know, to the growth of his body. To this end the body elemental or body mind takes over at birth (possibly even at the conception of the babe) and carries on thereafter, only occasionally interrupted by or interfered with by the head mind as that in turn develops. The body mind has things pretty much its own way during childhood. Following on puberty, the head mind begins to take over, at any rate in the outer self, and at this stage it is hustled along at an increasing rate by undergoing a process called education. In a competitive world, education's object is the proper one of teaching the child to earn a living. All the while the body mind, far from being really dispossessed, is watchfully biding its time, assimilating into its unfading memory all that passes through the head mind, and making it part of itself. All would be well if only affirmative, constructive thoughts reached it, if only healthful things were stored away in the subconscious. But it is not so; for fearful and destructive thoughts abound, and the body mind does not discriminate. All this conglomeration is kept in bond – until, should the accumulation of ill-health thoughts exceed the accumulation of good-health thoughts, the body duly becomes sick, and this with the same certainty that two and two make four.

We can always prove the spiritual law for ourselves: for if spiritual light can really penetrate and pervade the life of man it will surely transfigure it. So the answer is simple. Yet perhaps not so simple, for we have yet to face the problem of awakening the mind in the heart, after perhaps many years of imprisonment and neglect. It is unlikely that our innate divinity can all at once prove itself strong and resolute to transform lives.

According to the biblical recipe, human redemption comes about by constant prayer, repentance and fasting. For prayer and repentance substitute wiser living, wiser eating, wiser thinking, relaxation, wiser activities; for fasting substitute living more simply, and we have it. For if the real cause of our complaints is some inherent darkness working out in the body as illness, and the cure is the healing of man's soul, the only physician having power to effect such a cure on a universal scale is the Christ in man.

God's power can accomplish any healing; and in the degree that God is found so can a sufferer find the universal cure for all sickness. Every resource of medicine, surgery, nature cure, Christian Science, faith healing, has its failures as well as successes. With God there can be no failing. Only we may fail God, in which case God cannot cure us. It is this lurking but very real doubt in us all which qualifies what we read. We may feel sure about God but are very doubtful about ourselves, and with some justification.

Some of us are ignorant of the powers for self-healing inherent within ourselves; we sink into illness because somewhere lurking deep within us is the will to become ill; somewhere down by our solar plexus (where the body mind thinks and feels) there can grow up an affinity with, a leaning towards sickness. This must all be changed to will towards God, which is will towards health. Even when ill, by dogged force of will man can make himself continue to 'tick over'. This is not a cure, however. But if he can constantly reinforce that will of his by the will of God, then he can ask of God what he requires. Steadily, devotedly, with constancy, faith and trust, day in, day out, year in, year out, he can win back his health and happiness, this being the very course of action God wishes him to take.

White Eagle's words all point towards this conclusion:

'Disease means that the physical cells are out of alignment and out of harmony. This applies to all physical disability, even so-called accidents – all are manifestations of the failure of the physical cells to remain attuned to God.

'Medically you can call it any name you like, but whatever name you call it, the cause is the same, and the power which heals is the same. It is the power of God, and the power of God uses many channels on earth to heal, to repair the life, to open the spiritual vision, to develop the character and to bring the soul of man at last into the realisation of God. Always think in terms of spirit, the life of the spirit, the purifying power of the spirit.

'To preserve the physical body in health, harmony, joy and love, means that you must live in accordance with natural and divine law; when natural and divine laws are broken, the physical body suffers. So strive to become attuned to the Infinite, to live purely at every level. Seek always the life of the spirit.'

Probably there are those who would not agree with this diagnosis of the woes of mankind. They will doubtless feel that this outline of soul salvation and bodily healing has one inescapable disadvantage – that it will involve constant effort. How true! Cures of this nature will hardly bear comparison with, say, a series of injections, a course of drugs or massage, or possibly a minor operation. Methods which can cure without much effort will be the sufferer's choice. But no real healing can be obtained without effort. Neither will the good Lord do the job in its entirety while the patient sits idle, should spiritual healing be the method of cure. Things just don't work out that way. The rule seems to be payment for services received. Therefore the patient will have to earn his healing by giving something of himself as his personal contribution; for personal sacrifice in some form is a vital part of the transaction.

Here is a minor illustration of our theme, which takes the form of a letter:

'I have been asked to tell of a healing which I have had, for this is how I regard it. It all began many years ago. When I was sixteen I took to smoking a pipe, under the impression that it was a rather manly thing to do. For some forty odd years afterwards I smoked continually, perhaps averaging three ounces of tobacco weekly during that period. I was thus a fairly heavy smoker. During that forty years I made two big efforts of will power to break myself of the habit, and once gave it up for two years by sheer dogged mental force. During all that time the craving to smoke never left me, but nagged away like toothache. Then in my late fifties I began to read White Eagle's messages pretty assiduously, and found that after a time they seemed to get right inside me – into my real inner self, I mean, giving me a happier feeling. All the while I was still smoking, with never a thought of giving it up again. Then presently a new awareness about smoking came, partly bodily, partly of the spirit. I mean that my senses of smell, taste, and so forth got keener. I remember one day going to a cupboard and taking out a suit I had not worn for some time. It stank of stale tobacco, and I remember wondering whether all my clothes smelt like that; and then put it out of my mind. Oddly enough, although I was smoking away quite happily, my sense of smell began to object more and more to other people's tobacco! Also I got a new slant on things, I used to think it looked rather manly to smoke. Now I wasn't so sure, and wondered why people went about with pipes and cigarettes stuck in their faces. Then one day I thought how silly they looked!

'Not that all this was enough to make me give up smoking myself. The thing had gone too deep. But spiritually I wasn't feeling too good about it, having begun to realise that a man's body was, or should be, the temple of his soul – and that one didn't smoke in temples. So there it was, just a vague uneasiness gradually taking hold.

'Then all of a sudden it just happened. I took out my pouchful of tobacco and laid it on the fire. It was done quite deliberately, and not on impulse. Calmly I watched it burn away, although it was a shocking waste, seeing what tobacco cost. Thereafter smoking was finished for me. Never again did I have any desire to smoke.

'I was in my sixties when this happened. Having given it up I felt a sense of relief and even of freedom. Certainly I have been better in health since, and shall probably live a good few years longer. That is by the way, however. The main thing is that I have escaped from something which had become wrong – for me.'

The foregoing serves our purpose because it indicates how a constant reading of White Eagle's words stirred something in the heart mind of the reader, and how it led to a gradual refining of his bodily senses. The heart mind gradually reconditioned the body mind of the smoker and broke down the habit (no, the ritual, which is something much stronger) of forty odd years, so that a complete cure resulted.

It will at once be argued that this case proves nothing. Smoking cannot be properly classed as a disease. But that, surely, is a matter of opinion? Certain it is that it shortens life, that it induces minor and major complaints, that it might therefore be described as a long-distance killer. Might it not be described as a disease of the mind which externalises itself upon the body, at first in catarrhal afflictions and later in something more serious?

It is freely admitted that certain matters mentioned here are unprovable. They must depend on their innate reasonableness for acceptance. Others can be substantiated by some incident which illustrates the matter in question. Here is a story in point, written by the healer concerned with the cure, which happened some years ago.

Report on Mrs X

'I conversed for some time with this patient, so that I might get a good idea of the cause of her illness. A woman of around fifty, she had been a widow for many years. Her mind was clear and resolute. In childhood, it appeared, she was both neglected and ill-treated over a long period. This may have accounted to some extent for her condition.

'She had been a sick woman for a number of years, during which she had been unable to work or support herself. She had been under medical care and supervision during this period, being treated by doctor after doctor, and going from hospital to hospital. Harley Street was deeply interested in her case. For some time she had been under the care of a leading psychologist, of whose patience and devotion she spoke in the highest terms.

'None of the experts could discover the cause of her illness, nor indeed could they discover anything wrong with her physically. Neither did treatment by the psychologist have any success; over the years there had been a progressive decline in her health.

'When I first saw her she was very thin, unable to stand for very long, desperately pale, and her voice almost inaudible from weakness. Literally she was dying on her feet, and from no known disease. My own opinion was that here was a soul which had become separated from God. I believe that everybody has a link, strong or weak, with their Creator. Some are conscious of that link. It must be maintained in part at least or the person must die. Here I felt the link was so weak as to be almost non-existent, this is why no apparent physical cause for her illness could be found.

'As a spiritual healer my treatment was to contact the divine power and to pour it into her body. All spiritual healing is done in this manner; everyone has centres in the etheric body, or points of entry specially receptive to the healing rays. I concentrated on these, praying that the spiritual light might flow through my hands into this light-starved body and soul. When the treatment was over I left her sleeping on the healing couch, and an hour later she was still asleep. When awakened she seemed dazed and bewildered, and it was some time before she recovered sufficiently to go home. A few days later she wrote saying that she was feeling much better and happier as a result of this first treatment, and pleading for more help. She continued to come for treatment and in the end was completely cured, although her cure was not rapid – her twenty years of disability ensured that. In all my experience, I have never met a soul so divorced from its natural source of power and life, or so near its passing for this reason.'

This story has a special value because it gives so clear an illustration of what can happen to a soul cut off from its source of spiritual supply. Most of us think we live to ourselves alone, and are content to remain so, except in moments of desolation and despair. Yet in truth we are dependent on our Creator for every heartbeat, for every breath we breathe, and God is as necessary to us as air and sunlight. Indeed those two are of minor importance compared to the greater reality that is God.

7

THE NEW AWARENESS

To break spiritual and natural laws and then to expect the spirit agents to protect you means that you are challenging the Lord your God. This can be a grievous sin. When thus tempted say, 'Get thee behind me, Satan.' We have first to learn how to live in harmony with spiritual and natural law, and then we can look to our guardian angels for help on life's journey.

W.E.

The letter from the heavy smoker, towards the end of the last chapter, stressed the new awareness which came to its writer because of his quickening heart mind. He said that now he saw things from an entirely new angle. The moorings of his personal self were shifting from their anchorage in body and head mind because he was now sounding the depths of heart mind. As soon as this process begins, the body itself begins to change, undergoing a refining process which can eventually render it immune from bodily illness. Together with the shedding of the coarser physical atoms or substance of the body, and its replacement by more refined substance, comes new awareness of the great antiquity of this heart self of man. The man functioning with body and head minds only may scoff at the idea of survival after death, and may deride any suggestion that he needs many lives to educate and discipline himself properly and to awaken his heart mind; but once the heart mind quickens the man grows more contemplative and more tolerant, more visionary, more receptive to spiritual truth. Welling up from within comes the realisation that there is that in him which is eternal, far older than his transient outer man.

White Eagle says: 'Life has meaning and purpose, and that purpose is a spiritual one. Don't let yourself become so weighed down by things of every day (which are really unimportant because they are by their very nature transient) that you forget the eternal life of God.

'It is not easy at first to trust, and to hold fast to the inner light and truth of the heart. The body seems so solid, heavy and intractable and the mind so wayward. But the mind must become the tool of the spirit, and the substance of the body can be lightened, refined and uplifted by aspiration and by your love and devotion to God. This constant dwelling in the presence of God will come to mean more to you than anything else in your life. *But seek ye first the kingdom of God . . . and all these things shall be added unto you.* Then man will develop true humility, for he will realise that of himself he is nothing, can do nothing, but the God within him is the power which accomplishes all good. The God within him urges him to live, act and love according to divine law. Divine Intelligence is just, perfect and true, and can make no mistake; but while God's law is exact, there is also the mercy of God, the loving wisdom which softens the karma the soul makes for itself, and uses it to bring ultimate blessing to the soul. Try to accept the fact that all the difficulties and sorrows of your life are serving a wise purpose and even sickness or infirmity have the power to draw you closer to God.

'If you are sick – look into yourself; examine yourself deeply and truly. Be honest enough to try to recognise what particular weakness deep within yourself has really caused your illness. Once you can bring out this knowledge into the light of day you will have gone a long way towards curing yourself. It is good to do this because some day every soul will have to learn to look unflinchingly into the mirror of his own soul and see his true self revealed. Accept, then, that present suffering can teach something of infinite value to your future. Be sure also that illness regarded in this way can prove a good friend. . . .'

There is purpose in all suffering
'There may be some here who are sad because of the sufferings of those they love. It is very hard to have to remain still, to be unable to do anything. Whenever you witness suffering of the body or of

the mind which you are unable to heal, try to remember that the sufferer is working through a condition of life which will eventually bring the soul into the light. For any soul which suffers in the body is moving forward to join that heavenly host, of whom it has been said: *These are they which came out of great tribulation, and have washed their robes, and made them white in the blood of the Lamb.* So it is your work, ever to hold your beloved friend or dear one in that light, that hope, that courage which will help his soul to make good. We assure you that the Great White Spirit is a God of infinite love and tenderness. Nevertheless, every child of God is ordained to go through experiences on earth which will bring it into that happiness and peace for which it longs.

'We give you this message as one of hope, and to comfort you. For what takes place in the personal life, in the individual and particular life, is taking place in the collective life. That which you see in the world which appears painful is the way that the race must travel. That which you see in the personal suffering of someone is the way that that particular soul must travel.'

These words bring up the age-old problem of innocent suffering, which has baffled philosophy and religion throughout time. Yet it is as well to raise this problem because nothing has as yet been said about the graver and more pitiless complaints which afflict mankind; for as we know only too well, unhappy things can brood and breed down in that secret body mind where thoughts and feelings go into storage.

By these feelings are meant subconscious jealousy, irritability, envy, nagging anxieties and lowering apprehension, long-term resentments of which the unfortunate host is sometimes largely unconscious. Habitual irritability, for example, can grow into a subconscious continual soreness with life in general. Folk who can often organise and arrange their own home or business life to perfection wholly neglect their own inner life; and it is this inner life which largely determines whether or not they will live happily or the reverse. The body mind records it all, and never forgets.

Down in the heart mind is stored away yet another record, and this record represents either our credit balance or our overdraft with the recording angel – or, in other words, the good or bad karma which we have brought over to our present incarnation. Thus illnesses can arise either from karma incurred during a present life, or else they may be brought over from some seed sown in a previous life or lives. In this connection some extracts from talks given about cancer as long ago as 1938 are included. White Eagle then said:

'You have asked us to speak about cancer, your question being whether cancer is curable by surgery. When we explain that cancer arises from some deep-seated inharmony in the soul of man, you will understand the logic of our reply – that it is impossible to cure the disease purely by surgery. But cancer is not incurable. I would describe it as primarily a spiritual disease because it is largely brought about through inharmony due to the breaking of natural and spiritual laws (not necessarily in the present life). These laws may have been broken in ignorance, but it is through the suffering brought about by ignorance that the soul eventually passes into the land of light.

'We see this disease lodged in dark patches, or in a dark web, which is woven into the etheric body. In advanced stages we see very dark and almost solid masses in the etheric body. If by the surgeon's knife the offending growth is cut out, the diseased conglomeration has certainly been removed from the physical body. But we have not made a cure. The cancer still permeates the body in the blood stream, so is intimately associated with the etheric body, and with the ego.

'. . . The ego is the innermost, the impersonal self. The ego desires lessons. It does not mind how it gets them – *it wants the lessons.* This divine urge in each would grow and expand, even through pain. It desires to grow, first and foremost, in God consciousness, and knows it can only grow through knowledge gained by experience. This sounds rather remorseless, perhaps; but the ego will cause suffering in the physical body if there be no other way. You will ask, "What of the poor soul that is innocent, and does not understand why it is suffering?" It is true that the *mind* may be ignorant, but in the soul there is wisdom. If you were able to watch the process of spiritual enlightenment which can take place in the sufferer you would thank God for the gift of suffering. You would realise it still more could you watch that soul passing onwards to its reward. Remember, there are compensations. . . . Compensation is one of the great laws – one of the five great laws of life.

'If we say that the surgeon's knife will not cure cancer, what next? There is a cure, as common as air or water. I will describe it as a life essence. . . . This life essence is to be found in different forms and in different degrees throughout creation. Disease in the patient is due to a hold-up, or a blockage in the intake of the life essence. The perfectly harmonious, well poised, perfectly adjusted body and soul is ever open to its inflow.

'The essence is to be found, generously, prolifically, in some forms of vegetation. It is also present in rays of light and colour, which will be largely used some day in the treatment of cancer. Not all patients will respond to light and colour, however. Some need this life essence in a different form. It can be given in certain foods – vitalising and life-giving foods; or can be extracted and administered from the mineral kingdom. No one set cure is suitable for all sufferers, and the patient's response will be in accordance with his state of spiritual evolution. The crux of the whole lies in his quality of consciousness, and that quality is something brought over from his past.

'Long, long ago, when people lived closer to nature, they had perfected a method of obtaining all their healing from nature. They drew rays of light and colour from their surroundings. The Egyptian priests, for instance, made use of occult or spiritual rays in their healing. Even when an accident happened, the priests could assist nature to heal a wound rapidly. Today, you cleanse and dress an injury, and then say, "Let nature do its own work." The priest in Egypt or Central America applied invisible rays of healing, to heal the wound more rapidly.

'Since cancer is mainly the product of inharmony, this inharmony may work out either on the mental or physical planes or on both; and sometimes in the soul life. The reason for the growing incidence of this disease, so far as we can see, is because of the increasing artificiality of the life man is forced to lead. You will perhaps argue that it is wrong for the victims to suffer in this way when they know nothing about having violated spiritual law, or even that any such law exists. Spiritual law takes no account of ignorance: the law is just, perfect and true. Although from an earthly point of view the innocent seem to suffer, from the spiritual viewpoint there is no such thing as innocent suffering; moreover, if you could see with the eyes of spirit, you would see that a wonderful process of cleansing is taking place in the soul undergoing that suffering.

'We must bear in mind that the law of karma is the controlling force of every incarnation. If at some time there has been "sin against the Holy Ghost" (some people may understand this) a seed of darkness will lie within the soul, and this must be worked out and eliminated. This process may take the form of deep-seated disease, or it may take other forms not necessarily physical. Whatever discipline that soul requires will be brought to it in the form of opportunities or lessons which will enable it to acquire the quality of consciousness for which it is yearning. So, whenever a complete cure of cancer or other so-called incurable disease takes place, whether by operation or by some other method, it is because the sufferer has expiated his karma, perhaps unknown to himself, and the angels working under the Lords of Karma have repaired the injury done to the body.

'Fear, hate, resentment – all these are broken harmony. But resentment is not the only or even the main cause. Anything consistently inharmonious in the life may predispose the body to illness. If you will attune yourself to the Great White Light, to the eternal harmonies of life, there will be no cancer. Practise the laws of purity and godliness; eat clean food always;* breathe fresh air, drink only pure water and fruit juices; breathe in the great harmonies of nature; rest, sleep and work harmoniously without tension, rush, fear or anxiety; attain and hold fast to that serene and tranquil life lived by all who have mastered their lower self; don't let your emotional self be consumed by desire

---

* It has been computed that were the nation to become vegetarian the death rate from cancer would be at least halved. Facts and figures about this point would probably be illuminating, were they available.

and demands: all these must be controlled if you would grow healthy, whole and wise. Those who will attain great age live close to nature, close to God, and have peace.'

It is worth noticing that medical science too has concluded that cancer may have deep-seated mental and emotional causes. One more step in the same direction and medicine will find out that what applies to cancer applies also to every disease – that all disease originates from causes deep in the life history of the person concerned.

This brings us back to the case of Mrs X, touched on in the previous chapter. The mere telling of such a story leaves one in the air, so to speak. One can find little reason for her sufferings, and always there comes the nagging question as to why she should have suffered at all. Why should any soul find itself cut off from a merciful God, and by reason of lack of the light of God slowly decline? Surely the thwarted childhood of this person is an additional reason why she needed the love of God? For what reason under heaven is this or that man born blind, or deaf, dumb, crippled or handicapped? Why does accident and disease take such a toll of human life? Why do a thousand and one grievous questions which have always been the despair of churches, moralists and philosophers alike, chill our ardour when we are searching for God and want to trust Him? Can a blind and un-reasoning faith in God provide any satisfactory answer? Is an undaunted and unwavering faith, often in defiance of reason, the only resource of the would-be believer? Let us set ourselves to find the answer.

8

THE PUPIL AT SCHOOL

*Man was created in God's own image. The conception of man
made perfect is within the mind of God, is part of God. And
you, my brother, my sister, you are that perfect conception of
the child, the son of God, held within the mind of the Father-
Mother.*

W.E.

Far down beneath man's outer thoughts and feelings are some
certainties which are an integral part of him. Only if we look
deeply into the recesses of our nature do we discern their existence.

Among those certainties and waiting to surprise us is the ingrained belief that we shall continue to live on after death. Man
was once persuaded into believing that even his body would
rise from the grave. He has discarded that belief now, and accepts
that death will claim his body. But not the deeper mind of the
heart, the feelings and emotions which are his soul. This inner
man survives, and knows it will survive. Some people never
doubt this; with others it is a dim, almost unrecognised hope or
feeling. The strength or weakness of that feeling possibly depends on the preponderance of qualities in that soul which are
capable of survival. It is likely that those people whose interests
mainly centre around things of time and sense have less awareness
of survival than those who have followed their Master's injunction
to store up their treasures in heaven. . . . This does not altogether
explain why so many people shy away from any talk of religion,
or survival, or death – they find these subjects embarrassing. This
may be because really to believe in survival people have to
modify their outlook on daily life profoundly, and such a complete
change in outlook can be painful, and therefore unacceptable.
Nevertheless, deep down in us all, however much the head mind
disregards and denies it, is a profound certainty that something

64

in us survives – we just can't imagine ourselves turned into nothingness. How true is that instinctive conviction!

The acknowledgment of the soul's immortality faces us with another truth – and for many, less acceptable. Here let White Eagle speak, and we are quoting now from the book, Spiritual Unfoldment I*.

Man lives many lives
'Much confusion exists concerning this great principle or law of reincarnation. Some feel reluctance or repugnance at the very thought of having to reincarnate in a physical body, and cannot understand why, having passed through this physical life and on to the spheres of light, they should be forced to return. There seems to be no reason or logic in this law, and it does not fit in, they say, with their conception of an all-wise and all-loving God.

'They think of some beloved friend's passing, his returning from time to time bearing messages and descriptions of the heavenly places in which he lives, and they wonder why, once released, he must be drawn back again to the sorrow of earth life. There seems to be no sense in it. If the soul has absorbed so much of the heavenly light, it seems inconceivable for it to be reborn in lowly or perhaps uncongenial conditions on earth: a transgression of the divine order of love and progress.

'Reincarnation is a vast subject and we assure you that the ideas prevailing present but a crude and inadequate description of what really takes place. Until you clearly understand the law of re-incarnation, most of the deeper problems of life will remain obscure, and you will fail to find justice in life, even though you believe that God is good, all-wise and all-loving. Life is growth, the whole purpose of life on earth is spiritual growth, and there are universal problems which can only be answered by gaining understanding of the process of the soul's evolution. Man, con-fined by finite mind, has no conception of the true meaning of time. He thinks of three score years and ten, or indeed of a century, as a long period, when in truth it is but a flash. He does not think of incarnation in relation to the whole of life, and

* SPIRITUAL UNFOLDMENT I, White Eagle Publishing Trust.

because of this he fails to grasp how little can be gleaned from one short period of earth life.

'Let us then first consider a human life of three score years and ten; let us consider that one birth, life, and death; then let us compare the life of any ordinary man or woman with the life of godliness expressed by one of the great teachers or masters. Take the comparison between the two right home, and examine well your own soul. How many times have you fallen short of your own ideal? It is true that you are human, but you are also divine, and the purpose of life is the full development of divine manhood or the Christ man: indeed the purpose of creation is that all the sons of God may develop into the fullness and glory of the Christ.

'It is sometimes said: "Oh, so and so is an *old* soul!" But how has that soul become wise and strong and radiant? By reason of the discipline of the physical life. Discipline spells growth, and the finest discipline ordained by God, the Father-Mother, is the daily round, the common task.

'And yet every soul struggles against it. You will say: "Yes, we can accept this, but does not the soul have greater opportunities on the astral plane for development?" To a certain degree it does; but remember, the limitations of time and space, the restrictions of physical life, are removed on the next plane; therefore there cannot be discipline of the same nature, and the purpose of re-incarnation is discipline. To bear sorrow bravely, to meet success with a humble heart, to share happiness with others can discipline the life.

'The true home of the soul is in the celestial realms, a place of beauty and of bliss. Young souls without earth experience may be likened to babes lying in the womb; they have yet to learn to use their limbs, to kick, to walk and to act. We must remember also that those babes are potential Gods, young creators. God devised physical existence as a means of training the child to use all its faculties.

'We can think of no better symbol of man's earthly life than that of the seed planted in the darkness of the earth in order that it may grow into the perfect flower. The perfect flower, the archetypal flower, is created first in the mind of God. and then the seed is planted in the earth to grow to fullness. So is it with you, who are as seeds planted in physical form to grow towards the light until you become perfect sons and daughters of God – the perfect archetypal God man which God held in His mind in the beginning. . . .'

The greater self
'Conceive first then the soul of man, not as you know it in the personality of everyday life, but as something far greater, which dwells in the heaven world and is an aggregate of all the experience of past incarnations. Personal man represents only a small part of the greater soul which dwells in a higher state of consciousness, although the personality can live in greater or lesser degree in touch with that greater soul, and can draw from it if it will.

'Man, then, possesses a soul in the heaven world which contains the seed, the spirit, the very essence of God in man which directs the course of life. That is why we say that *God directs the path of life*. That urge which stirs man to the highest, sometimes against the will of the lower mind, or the self will, is the God within man. And it is this spirit or divine spark which directs the life of the soul, guiding it through many earthly experiences. Each time a part of the soul descends into incarnation it absorbs certain forms of experience necessary for the growth and evolution of the greater soul above. So, according to your growth and development you contribute to that larger self. As you strive on this earth plane in succeeding incarnations you are building that beautiful soul.

'We would enlarge your conception of reincarnation so that you discard the idea of man bobbing backwards and forwards between two worlds. We want you to get a larger, grander idea of the continual growth of God consciousness taking place within the greater soul which is yours. Sometimes when in deep trouble or distress you may receive a flash of power and light from that self and accomplish or endure something you had previously thought impossible. Or it may be that others known to you have received a like flash, by which the coward has risen to be a hero, the selfish to become selfless. You have no conception of man's potentialities once he can make and hold the contact with that greater self which is his true being.

'Never make the mistake, beloved children, of judging any man: never look at a soul and say, "Poor thing, it is unevolved," for you do not know what you say. It may be that he who appears degraded is a soul of purity and great beauty in the heaven world. You cannot judge. . . .'

Why can we not remember?
'You may ask what proof we can give you of the theory of re-incarnation. We answer that spiritual things can only be proved in a spiritual way. Few can give proof of reincarnation (although there are a number of proven instances of it) or indeed any other spiritual truth; but proof will come to you through your own intuition, as a result of your own experience.

'The only way that man can attain knowledge of the divine secrets is through the path of love and selflessness. Mind (which has its place in evolution) can never of itself unfold the truth; but it is necessary for the mind to be developed before compre-hension can dawn. Man seeks to find truth through much reading, but the heart of truth lies in the spirit, and only you can find truth for yourself – no one else can give it to you. In your search for a clear understanding of reincarnation you must become acquainted with the man within, your innermost self. When you come face to face with your innermost self you no longer cry for proof: the path of the soul's evolution is known.

'You may wonder too why you cannot remember the past; but can you recall the time when you were aged two, three or four? How then can you hope to recall incarnations of hundreds and thousands of years ago? Memory is not in the physical brain, nor can it be found in the astral or the mental bodies with which you have clothed yourself. But when you can function in the higher body, which some call the causal body, and which I will call the temple, your vision will be opened and you will remem-ber, because you will touch the celestial mind, which is the store-house of all the past.

'How long elapses between each incarnation? We cannot lay down any hard and fast rule. We cannot say that man reincarnates every two, three or five hundred years. That would be wrong. If we tell you that man passes out of one body into another immediately we shall be wrong again. If we say that thousands of years elapse between each incarnation we shall still not be giving the whole truth. All depends upon the individual. But it is possible for a soul to reincarnate quickly for a special purpose.

'At what stage does the soul enter the body? Is it before or at the time of birth? We would say that the soul gradually merges itself into the body as the years advance. At about the age of twenty-one the soul has generally incarnated in full, although we would prefer not to bind ourselves as to time. Contact by the soul with the body of the mother is made before physical conception.

'Another question you may ask is, whether it is possible for the soul to retrogress in any one incarnation? We would say that if one misses something beautiful on the road it is advisable to re-trace one's steps to find it. Would you call that retrogression? But always remember that it is impossible for one soul to judge another: to judge is to condemn yourself.

'You may also ask whether reincarnation is always into the same family and, if so, whether with the same parents and the same children. No, but members of the same family tend to draw together. The link in fact may sometimes be that of brother or sister, father or son, husband or wife. You are bound by the links of karma both to family and friends, and you tread the evolutionary path together in families and groups. According to your karma you will find love and happiness waiting for you; or perhaps enmity and discord, which it will be your task to change into love.'

'By his incarnation man is bound to affect that part of the world in which he dwells; such is the law. Man is placed where he may give most nourishment to physical life. He gives and also receives nurture from the earth life.

'We do not wish to force the truth of reincarnation upon the reluctant. Nevertheless reincarnation, like life and death, is a law;

whether a man believes it or not makes no difference. It is a little strange that some people seem to think that by saying they do not believe in survival after death, reincarnation or the law of cause and effect, they abolish them.

'We stress, however, that man has free will. He is never constrained or coerced, never withdrawn from heaven and cast back to earth willy-nilly. So long as a man declares, "I do not want to return," the answer comes: "Well, my child, rest awhile; there is no hurry." God never hurries. It is all a question of the evolution of the individual soul, and when you have reached understanding your one longing will be to get back into harness; your one question, how soon you can go.

'We have already suggested that you may tend to think that the soul might learn its lessons and work out its salvation on the astral plane, and that on that plane it will come up against exactly the same kind of conditions as on the earth. But the substance of the astral plane is very different from that of matter. It is more easily moulded by, more malleable to thought. In dark, dense physical matter the soul comes up against a severe lesson, which must be mastered and can only be mastered *in matter*. The whole purpose of creation is spiritual evolution: the soul must master dense matter. It must become wholly master of dense matter because it has within it the God life, and God is working in matter throughout His own creation. The God within grows and evolves until it has completed its work, which is absolute mastery over its environment. It is easier, much more comfortable, to think of the soul passing away from the bondage of the flesh into another world and working out its salvation in nicer and easier conditions; but it does not happen to work that way.

'We would also like to point out that the joy which comes to a soul who attains mastery over the flesh is incomparable. If we could only convey something of that intense joy of accomplishment gained through physical experience you would then fully understand and rejoice in the opportunities given to the soul to return to earth for fresh adventure.

'Many of you have returned to earth because you want to help humanity, not necessarily by going to church and doing good works, but because your very presence in life can be a joy and comfort to those about you; to the family into which you were born, to the family of which you may later become a parent, and to many friends as well. You can serve best, not by scattering your energies and forces, but by *being* a son of God, and by giving warmth and light to help each flower bloom its best in the particular patch of garden in which it is planted. . . .'

Angels of light and darkness★
'There are two aspects of life called respectively good and evil. On the one side, the good, are many beings working under the direction of our Lord and Master Christ. On the other are hosts who are called evil, or angels of darkness who, although their work is different from the angels of light, are still working within the law of the cosmos, God's law. If you accept God as a Father of infinite power, you must recognise that what is called evil (or that which comes within the sphere of the angels of darkness and destruction) is yet within the hand and under the control of the Infinite Power. Otherwise there would be absolute chaos; otherwise you could have no faith, no confidence, no trust in that divine love which has been preached to mankind through the schools of mystery teaching, which in their turn have fed the religions throughout the ages. Always there has been revealed to the true pupil of the master an infinite love, guiding, protecting, inspiring and bringing good out of apparent chaos.

'But surely if there are both angels of light and angels of darkness constantly at work, this must mean that conflict will never cease? It is all a question of one's conception of light and darkness. We are inclined, do you not think, to lay too much stress on darkness as something *opposed* to light? When we rise in spirit above the level of the earth we are surprised to learn that light and darkness are actually one, that conflict ceases and harmony reigns supreme, because light and darkness are reflections one of the other. Life cannot go on without darkness, which is necessary to evolution, providing as it does the negative aspect to set off the positive.

★ SPIRITUAL UNFOLDMENT II, White Eagle Publishing Trust.

'But you will not let us off with this! For you will ask whether there are *really* angels and forces of darkness; and whether God the creator is also God the destroyer. Yes, in a sense this is so. The God of darkness can be likened to Shiva of the Hindus – the destroyer; but that destructive element proves itself in reality to be constructive; the destroyer which sweeps away unwanted growths is actually preparing the way for rebuilding, for re-creation. The angels of darkness therefore have their place in the great scheme of evolution.

'We must establish this firmly and clearly in our minds; that while the angels of light are working under the supreme command of the Lord and Master of Light who is Christ the Son, the angels of darkness also are working within the law and under the command of God. But their work is complementary to that of the angels of light. These two forces are playing upon humanity with a definite purpose to bring about evolution, to bring man to the consciousness of his own innate godliness. For in the beginning the human spirit, the individual spark of divine life was breathed forth from God to descend through many stages of life until it became clothed in matter in order to learn to control matter, and so that the divine spark of unconscious godliness might grow into a God-conscious being. You have the example of man perfected in the divine consciousness in Jesus the Christ.

'Before humanity was sent forth upon this path of earthly experience, advanced beings came to this planet to assist mankind to become established on earth. Helping also with this process were angels of light and angels of shadows, principalities and powers of both good and evil. Let us restate the last sentence, saying angels *in* the light, angels *in* the shadows, angels serving the light and angels serving the darkness. The angels of light (or good) stand for the forces of construction; those of the shadows (or so-called evil) the necessary forces of destruction – necessary, because they are ever at work pruning away those aspects of individual and national life and thought which have outgrown their usefulness. Therefore do not think of the light and the dark angels as adversaries constantly at war, but rather as the one being the complement of the other. Neither underestimate the

power of these beings, for both aspects of angelic life are continually at work, through generation after generation, cycle
after cycle of earth's humanity, to assist the growth and destroy
that which is unworthy in man.

'The question then arises in your mind. Can the angels of
darkness, these angelic forces perhaps not yet fully aware of the
light and the power and the wisdom of the Most High, triumph
over the angels of light and thus cause the destruction of humanity?
Our answer is no. The dark angels can go so far and no further
because then they are caught up in a cosmic law which renders
them powerless. God does not allow the universe to slip out of
His hands. Nothing can happen outside the will of God.

'Two paths lie before man on earth, and he may choose which
one he takes. On the one hand he can work in harmony with
cosmic law – and the man who has attained the vision of the
heavenly mysteries always works in harmony with cosmic law,
with the law of love. On the other hand, he who is still in a state
of darkness works, albeit unconsciously, against the cosmic law.
Consequently he surrounds himself, through incarnation after
incarnation, with suffering. But as soon as man learns to live and
work in harmony with divine law, and to give himself con-
fidently to God, then he attains happiness. The angels of light
work with him, and he with them, and together man and angel
are able to assist in the unfolding of God consciousness in the
rest of humanity. . . .'

Love is the key to truth
'There is one basic truth from which all religions take birth – that
of man's innate divinity; of man's creation by the Father-Mother
God in order that the human child of God, the spirit of man,
may through divers incarnations grow from unconsciousness to
divine consciousness. And the one key which will eventually
unlock the gate of heaven to this child of earth is love. Love is
the keynote of all spiritual growth. It is one thing to talk about
love, but quite another to become truly loving, and the whole of
life is designed to bring forth such true love, though love in any
form is good. We who can look closely into the souls of men and

women see so much spontaneous kindness, so many gentle thoughts, so many helpful actions: these are godlike both in motive and effect – godlike, because the soul in that one moment is manifesting love, is manifesting God. Because of this, we are assured that some day every human life will grow to express love and kindness spontaneously to all God's creation.

'We have said that the divine life in man begins as a seed, which is separated from the divine Father-Mother and is planted in earth life, even as a garden seed is planted in its seed bed. When you begin to consider the beauty, the majesty, the radiance, the unimaginable glory of God, and then think how little the soul grows in one incarnation, you will realise the aeons of experience which lie before him before man can achieve his potential. Think of the average person you know; kindly and human as he may be, what major spiritual progress does he appear to make in the course of one brief life? Not very much, you will answer; and this may give you some idea of how long a period is required for such a soul to mature to mastership. And only through living in matter can the soul so evolve that it eventually attains such maturity.

'Many have found belief in reincarnation deeply satisfying, because it explains so much that is incomprehensible in human life. You can learn through this belief that all men are brethren at heart, all are of the one spirit. You can learn that the man who was king yesterday, or in some previous life, may be a beggar today; that he who was materially poor yesterday may be rich indeed tomorrow. Knowledge of reincarnation brings home the true values of life as opposed to the false values of the world. It offers repeated opportunity for happiness, enjoyment, learning, and all things dear to the heart of man. More than all it reveals an ever-present God of love and justice.

'You will ask if a soul always remains of the one sex through its many incarnations. We do not regard sex as you do. The soul is drawn to the body, either male or female, that will enable it to gain the particular experience it needs. It will usually reincarnate with its companions of former lives because it has again to contact those whom it loves, and also those to whom it owes debts, for every debt has some day to be repaid. Every day of your lives you are yourself making new obligations, new debts – which is a thought well worth consideration, for maybe it can reveal to you some opportunity now waiting. But remember also that you can so order your lives that you no longer contract bad debts; every bad debt must eventually be paid.

'When man really understands and accepts the law of reincarnation, he begins to understand something of the purpose of life. One short span of years with little or nothing accomplished would seem hardly worth its pain and trouble. But when at last the soul is able to understand whither its long, long journey is leading, it becomes filled with hope and happiness, knowing that whatever horrors it undergoes, whatever is withheld during one incarnation, is all for a wise purpose. When the vision clears at last, sorrow becomes a passing thing. The soul moves onward to greater and more glorious illumination; it feels the love of God quickening its very being. All the gifts of love are but God's gift to the soul. Every hope and aspiration of the spirit will be realised in God's time. This very thought brings all light, hope and joy! So, when the lower mind grumbles and says, "If only I could believe – it is all too nebulous!" refuse to listen. Put that earthly mind in its place, then your higher self, your higher mind, will grow and understand all. *Eye hath not seen, nor ear heard, . . . the things which God hath prepared for them that love him.* But understand that you have first to develop powers within yourself to enable you to comprehend and enjoy such glories. The way to develop these powers is to use wisely all the experiences life brings and learn to triumph over the lower self. This means gaining control over your environment and all its inharmonies. And *the light shineth in darkness*! And that light is within you. The light has to shine forth until darkness no longer exists. Then you are back again in the very heart of the Sun, the Source from which you originally set forth on a journey in the course of which you were destined to develop God consciousness and to learn to use the God qualities with which every son/daughter of God has been endowed.'

We know now that all illness originates from deep inharmonies within the soul of man; we know the cure for all illness lies in the restoration of harmony within that soul. How simply and plainly the whole scheme can be set forth; all that is needed for man's health and salvation is his surrender to the God power and the divine healing. How profoundly obvious does such a truth seem – and how supremely difficult will it be for the restless mind of man to make such a surrender.

Possibly the reason why most people dread the idea of re-incarnation is, understandably, that they feel so knocked about by the present life that they shrink from repeating the experience. Nevertheless, a vast majority of the human race in the East already believe that man must return not once but many times. Teachers such as Krishna, Gautama Buddha and Jesus gave out this truth to their followers; belief in reincarnation at the time of Jesus was so widely held in the East that almost automatically it became incorporated in the teaching of the early Christian Church. Study of the sayings of Jesus reveals his acceptance of reincarna-tion as the balancing factor in human life.

We have to assume that early Christianity possessed spiritual truths which the world found necessary to its well-being. It must have explained God and justified His ways to man. In other words, it must have been a reasonable religion which could withstand hard knocks. Some of the utterances of the early Fathers of the Church lead one to assume as much. Origen was one who not only accepted but said that apart from belief in reincarnation there could be no admissibility of divine justice. 'Wherein,' he asks, 'lies the explanation of the diversities of fate among rational beings?' Latin Fathers of the Church such as Nemesias, Synesias, and Hilarius took a somewhat similar attitude, and spoke of man-kind's fall to earth, and of the gross earthly bodies men must wear after their former state of blessedness; Justin Martyr wrote in much the same strain. Not until about the year A.D. 500 did the Fathers of the Church suppress the doctrine of reincarnation in these memorable words, 'Whoever shall support the mystical doctrines of the pre-existence of the soul, and the consequent wonderful opinion of its return, let him be anathema'.

By their suppression of the doctrine of reincarnation the Fathers of the Church made Christianity unreasonable – or at any rate made the professed Christian dependent on faith rather than on reason, when both should support him. Looking back over the centuries, it is grievous to recall that this one injunction robbed the Church of its power to explain the manifold apparent injustices of human life. Men see their kind sinning and apparently getting away with it; they watch the suffering of the seemingly innocent, and are harrowed by the problem of cruelty; they see children born blind, crippled, paralysed, or insane. Of all these an infinite Father seems heedless, and orthodoxy is powerless to explain them. All honour to those Christian lives which have done so and held fast to faith in God despite all! But need so severe a strain have been imposed?

What has all this to do with healing? Everything, since real sickness begins when man resents or is embittered by his world; and the beginning of all healing is peace of heart. We cannot live serenely until we glimpse why we are living, and where we are going. The beginning of understanding is the beginning of healing.

Need it be said again that the outstanding advantage a knowledge of reincarnation offers is that without it human existence remains incomprehensible and always will do so? Without it, neither morality, philosophy nor religion can explain or grapple with life's problems; or, at any rate, hitherto they have failed to do so. Because if the soul of man fails to survive death, his span of mortal life can only be regarded as a futile, incomprehensible and occasionally tragic episode. Nor will survival, of itself, sufficiently explain life. The man who wants to know what life is for realises that one single human existence is far too brief. Knowledge of reincarnation is therefore an essential complement to knowledge of survival. Man has an inherent sense of justice – and he can put up with much seeming injustice if he knows that in time a divine justice will right all wrong; he can bear even poverty, indignity, sickness, and calamity, when assured that somehow, somewhere, at some time these things will be righted. What can make life really sting is an acute sense of its unfairness. And, rightly understood, the idea of reincarnation can remove that sting.

Finally it is necessary to add that the higher world to which the soul of man goes when the body dies is a kinder, a more loving world, of which this life is but a shadow, and that any beauty here is but a foretaste of that beauteous world to come. Someone once said that what man wanted in the life beyond was not punishment but compensation. That is broadly what will happen; waiting for us is an existence compensatory to this. Over there life is gracious, lovely and serene; over there our loved ones are waiting. It is well worth striving for and winning such a reunion. But can man happily linger there for ever and a day when the world down here has such claims on his compassion and needs his help so sorely?

9

NEVER GROW OLD

How can man live as God created him to live, without conscious contact with the part of him that is spirit, with his celestial self? Such loss of contact, brethren, is the reason why you grow old. The reason why the body ages, decays and eventually passes away is that people fail to keep their contact with the spiritual life, with their spiritual self.

W.E.

By now it should be apparent that the process of self-healing here set forth contains nothing mysterious, but it does entail a great deal of hard work on oneself. The student, however, need not expect too much of himself all at once, nor need he struggle on wholly without assistance. Our next section describes some methods of healing designed to reinforce our efforts towards personal self-healing.

Such self-healing is vitally necessary. One has only to think of the multitude of hopelessly sick and bedridden, and of the money which is being spent without stint by the National Health Service and through private effort on restoring the sick (often only to a kind of half-life), to realise how sorely needed is such self-healing.

In the days of old they had another answer to the problem of sickness. People then resorted to the temple for their healing. They sought the help of their priest who showed them that their sickness was spiritual in origin. The priests were specialists in many different aspects of healing, but they began at the right end of their patient's disease – at the beginning of his complaint, with its source in his soul; and they began their healing by helping the patient to understand how his sickness had come about. The priests were trained men of great spiritual power. When they spoke, their patient listened and did not forget. The religion by which they bade him live was a hard-working, hard-wearing religion capable of withstanding hard knocks, and well suited to that age. The results were often amazing, for complaints which threatened months of sickness or early death were sometimes healed in a few hours.

There is a disease which kills more people with more certainty than any other. How shall we designate this dreadful complaint? Shall we call it the threescore years and ten bogey, or the premature old age complex? Neither seems quite to hit the mark. Let us try instead to list the symptoms of the complaint, which begins, say, round about thirty years of age with the appearance of the first grey hairs, or the first line on the face, the first bodily hint of creakiness indicative of the possibility of some day growing old. The symptoms accelerate with the passing years. Very soon comes the 'too old at forty' complex; and then the 'too old at fifty,' and finally then the 'far too old and due for death at seventy' complex.

Of course, all this talk of ageing, and this willing of oneself into premature old age comes as an absolute gift to the body mind, presenting it with its supreme opportunity for dramatising itself as old age personified through the medium of the body. So-called second childhood is of course an instance of the body mind repeating its former domination over the body. This is when childhood memories begin to flood back out of their store in the subconscious. These things happen when the head mind becomes dispossessed. Thus the body mind reaches the climax of its career, and prepares for its dramatic exit, while all the time the head mind meekly acquiesces. Yet this should never be! Man should suffer neither age, disease nor death in this way. It all comes about because of man's being only a two-thirds person, consisting of body and head mind. Let him become a whole man, equipped with body and head minds completed and balanced by the heart mind, and he can live long and healthily, simply because his body and being will by then be composed of finer substance, no longer subject to the coarser diseases. Here is no mystery – for this finer body possesses greater resistance and resilience, greater powers of re-creation, because it draws upon divine power. It is more durable than the physical body, thus old age holds few terrors for it. And when the time comes for that body to be laid aside the soul will peacefully disengage and transfer itself to brighter realms as gently and naturally as one falls asleep at night.

Rightly, no man or woman should suffer painful disease or painful death. Increasing years should grace and enhance a man's powers, enrich his heart and nature. True, there will come a natural and inevitable transfer of energies and vitality from body to man's higher self and this transfer should herald the finer part of a life's work; for the richest and most creative years of man's life should be the sixties, the seventies, and indeed the eighties. Why not, indeed, reach into the nineties and pass the century, and even onwards? A useful century of service is a worthy ideal which can be consummated by anyone given the will and purpose to do it. At any rate a century will do for a start. What limits us, and what ultimately shepherds us into the arms of death, is the old body mind idea that at some stated time we ought to die. The right and only time to die is when our period of usefulness to our fellows expires. White Eagle now speaks to us about the principles of true living.

Shaping up to life
'Events around you will ultimately shape the course of your life, try as you will to order them. Man, being constrained to bow to forces greater than himself, must ask himself how far does his power of free will operate? We answer that in one sense only is he absolute master of his fate: he may shape his future *by his reactions to events of the present.* If he takes hardly that which his karma brings, meeting it with anger, rebellion, bitterness, or by accepting defeat, he is inviting a repetition of that particular series of events; sooner or later he has to learn lessons which he is sometimes extraordinarily reluctant to accept.

'On the other hand, man can put aside his rebellious self, and even while suffering turn to look within, to ask in humility what lesson his sorrow comes to teach, what gift it offers, what treasure it may reveal. The measure of man's free will lies in his power to determine whether life shall sweeten or embitter him. By his actions and reactions now, he creates his future for good or ill. And always he can be helped. He is not alone in his struggle; always there is his guardian angel who can help him if only he will accept that help. We also help but we need your co-operation and prayers to assist us.

'Once man comprehends the great cosmic law of cause and effect, then he knows that any action or speech of his which is harmful to his brother will rebound like a boomerang upon himself. This law cannot be escaped. Usually you will see its outworking in your present life, but not always. You will not always understand what is happening. The most important thing, however, is to become so attuned that in every moment of your life you are creating or setting up a cause, which some day is bound to have an effect upon your body, your soul, and upon your life generally. Remember that karma, as it is called, not only presents you with a bill for a debt which is overdue, but at the same time offers you an opportunity; because through paying that account – in sorrow or sickness or regret – you, the spirit, the *real* you should have learned your lesson. If you refuse to learn, then the lessons mount up and are presented again and again. So we can truly say, accept all these opportunities disguised as so-called karma. Try to see, try to read the lesson which is being presented, and be thankful.

'But do not think that your complaint is sent to you by God. God never inflicts pain on anyone; but divine law decrees that any inharmony in the soul will eventually and automatically work itself out through the body. All life's experiences have but one object, to raise the whole being of man from mortality to im-mortality; to lift it up from the bondage of matter into heights of spiritual radiance.

'Your own part in becoming whole and healthy is to forget your symptoms and to concentrate instead on the Source of all life and light, whence alone can come peace and tranquillity of spirit. Set your heart resolutely on the things of God, the things of heaven, and all that is needed will be given to you. . . .'

Why be separate?

'It may help you to gain control over your mind if you remember that the Creator ever holds within His thought the creature He has created; the God who created you is continually holding you in His mind. You may think of God as being infinitely remote and impersonal, caring nothing for anyone so infinitesimal as yourself. You may completely forget God, but if God momentarily forgot you, you would be snuffed out of existence. Every second of your life you are closely held within the mind and heart of the Father-Mother God – what have you then to fear?

'Each human spirit is itself a God in embryo, a unit or concourse of tiny God cells, all in their innermost linked with God in constant at-one-ment; yet each cell endowed with the power to isolate itself from its fellows, though never from God.

'Once man fully realises that he is part of God, made in God's image, in His likeness, he will no longer think in terms of separateness for he will know that all are of the one spirit. He will no longer think in terms of here and there, but of an everywhere in which there can be nothing separate, no creature living only to and for itself; and in this consciousness of God and eternity, pain and death will no longer have any power to enslave him. . . .'

A few words about the power of thought

'The master, in sending you guidance, will always speak to you with love, and direct your thoughts towards good will and peace; never to antagonism, never to self-aggrandisement, but ever to humility, loving kindness and helpfulness to your fellow creatures.

'Man's thought creates; man's thought of today is externalised tomorrow. He thinks of war and disaster, and when his thought becomes strong enough it externalises itself on the physical plane. So it is with death. Remember that life is thought. God holds the universe in His thought. What you think, you become. What the world thinks today, it becomes tomorrow. What you have in your physical life lay first in the thought world. You will find when you leave your body that you are in a world of strong desires and passions, if you have so lived and thought; but the person whose thoughts are kind and loving and simply good, who lives day by day manifesting the spirit of Christ, according to his development and awakening to spiritual truth, will find himself in a world like that of his own thoughts. The difference is that now you can hide your thoughts by your body, so that very few people know what you are thinking. But when you pass to the spirit world you can no longer hide your thoughts, and that which you have been thinking, you find expressed or externalised in your new life. Leave your physical body and you will pass into a new world of great beauty; it can also be of great happiness – and you are the only one who can bar yourself from entering into this world.

'We want you to understand that your life here is always interwoven with your life in the spirit. As you are on earth, so you are here in the world of spirit, the world in which your guides and your loved ones live; they come back to love you, to help you, to lift you up when you are in despair. And incidentally, when you open yourself to this inner light, it begins to "iron away the creases". People grow old because of their emotions, the anxieties, the worries they permit to harrow them. Why do people grow sick? Because of emotional stress and strain, or overstraining of the body. If you were always attuned to the Great White Light, there would be no sickness.

'Spiritual healing is brought about by the power of spiritual aspiration; when the thoughts are truly aspiring, then the light of Christ, the rays of Christ, fall into the heart; and as soon as the rays of Christ are felt in the physical body, having great power they can reverse the order of things. Where the physical body is dark, light takes possession, dominating the body and controlling the physical atoms. This is how miracles are performed. When we say that thought has the power to do this, we of course mean divine thought, the thought which rises from a pure and aspiring heart. The power which comes when the heart is set upon God can reverse negative to positive, darkness to light; the inflowing of the light will produce perfect health because it will produce harmony.

'Don't fear the future. Don't fear the unknown, not even death itself. For with every forward step you take you are entering a fuller existence. Even if you lose your present body this only enables you to step forward into a world of light. Here on earth, by your thoughts, by your aspirations and your actions you are preparing yourself to awaken in a new world. Without right thought, without love you cannot awaken fully in the world of light because you will have no vision to see it. This is why you are always being told from the world of spirit to develop God qualities, Christ qualities here and now, so that as you step forward you will carry the light which will reveal the wonders awaiting you. And all the beauties of the spirit life which will be revealed to you emanate from your own soul.

'Within, my brethren, within is the light; give it forth. . . .'

Always work for harmony
'The main principle ruling life should be harmony, so never enforce too rigidly anything which your body would of itself reject or your mind resent. I remember a man who became very enthusiastic about vegetarianism, and hurriedly decided never to eat flesh again. He had arrived at that stage where he desired to discontinue flesh eating; but he did violence and hurt to his body by so rigorous and sudden a change. Work always for harmony and gradual soul growth – this is the better way. As the God consciousness grows in man so the body will, of its own accord, reject the killing of animals for its food because the auric content of the blood attracts undesirable elementals, and also because cruelty in any form is the antithesis of love; but while your body demands these things then eat, and bless God. Again, never hurt another's feelings by forcing on him your own views regarding diet. Even if you eat nothing but the right foods but still persist in thinking the wrong thoughts, of what good is your food to you? In course of time you will certainly get ill, despite all your care. It is not so much the food you eat, but what you think that matters.

'No man can attain perfect health without an inner awareness of the spirit of his Creator. You may indulge in all the nature diets that you like; you may breathe in the fresh air; you may drink only pure water; you may exercise your body and breathe deeply – all these things will help you to become more healthy. But remember, true health means holiness, and unless a man can attune himself to the Source of his life, to his Creator, he cannot become perfectly whole, perfectly balanced. A man must become perfectly balanced between heaven and earth if he is to be whole and healthy. . . .'

'I come in little things'

'Living as he does in a complex and possibly civilised age, man grows to expect too much pleasure out of too many things, and overlooks the place where true happiness is to be found. To find a sweet and wonderful happiness, a spontaneous joy, learn to love and wonder at the simple things; to love clear, starlight nights, the murmur of trickling waters, the wind in the trees, the perfume of the flowers and of the woods, and to be friendly with little furry animals. Learn to love the song of the birds and to absorb the beautiful colours of nature. All these are gifts brought by a wise Mother who is the bestower and origin of all natural life, beauty, and happiness.

'Rest quietly, knowing that the wise Mother and the infinitely loving Father are bringing the children of the present age through sorrows born of self will into the sunlight of good will and brotherhood, where they may live that perfect life which is prepared for all the vast family of God. Does all this sound too childlike, too impractical for you to accept? Maybe. Nevertheless it is the childlike things we need to cherish, to take us all back into the heart of happiness. . . .'

A friendly world

'When you go out for a walk, don't go forth tightly wrapped up in yourself but look out on a very friendly world, seeing it as intensely active, full of interesting things. Observe, take due heed of all that you see, and store away in the treasury of memory a fund of beauty. Train yourself in this constant observation of nature. Take in your hand a rose, blessing and loving it as God's gift to you, sent to you by His sunshine and His rain. Quietly observe its form and fragrance, and inhale the very essence and soul of that flower. Think of the human care and devotion which has brought this rose into being, and bless someone's brotherly act of service – for all labour is service. Feel your brotherhood with this flower – feel that in you and in the rose pulses the same life essence. . . . Enter into the heart of the rose and so learn how this peace, purity and fragrance can arise out of earthliness – a peace and sweetness born of light, remember. Let the beauty and fragrance of the rose find a dwelling place in you. . . .'

Accidents

Someone will be sure to ask some time why accidental injuries or death by accident come about. The questioner will want to know how accidents can happen if this universe is fundamentally controlled by a divine law and order. Well, a complete answer exists. But whether it can be made clear is another matter, for some things are simply beyond human capacity to comprehend. For one has first to forget this world of hard physical substance and think of it as an eddying thought world in which currents of thought turn and whirl and race hither and thither faster than the speed of light, and in which nothing is real except thought. In such a world, which seers declare (and science begins to believe) is nearer reality than our world of the physical senses merely, man has his real being. As he walks the streets, continual thought currents whirl about him, among them those which he himself generates and contributes. Some are harmful, some beneficial; some can do him damage, others can help him. Day and night, year in, year out, he lives principally in such a world of thought, of which he himself is a partial creator.

Let us consider what happens to the violent angry thoughts such as man occasionally sends out, for instance when he thinks about potential enemies. In the recent past, when the nations made a habit of this sort of anger, when their press and propaganda inflamed their peoples, armaments piled up (armaments being war thoughts taking concrete form), and world war was the natural result. In other words, violent thoughts rebounded on their senders; like a boomerang they returned, possibly with their original violence augmented.

As with a nation, so also with individuals. Let a man indulge in violent thoughts, about, say, his neighbour, for long enough, and those same thoughts will duly rebound. As to the manner of their return, some will certainly take shape as an accident – and accidents can happen not only on the physical plane, but can be also emotional, social, or financial, taking the form of sudden misfortune or loss.

Another factor which appears to bring temporary disarray to an orderly universe is man's foolhardiness – *thou shalt not tempt the Lord thy God*, for assuredly foolhardiness is asking for trouble of some kind, and neither ignorance nor innocence seems to provide any excuse. Nothing is more certain than that if a man habitually tempts the Lord God (even blindly walking across a street, or by overworking or ill using his body in some way) sooner or later accident or misfortune will occur. On the subject of accident or sudden death, White Eagle has this to say:

'In all truth and sincerity we say that there is no such thing as accident. Accident is a method of passing. *There is a destiny which shapes our ends* – a destiny behind all the happenings of life. When man realises this, when he recognises the laws governing his physical and spiritual life, he will find true peace of soul. Nothing can happen outside the plan.

'The Great Architect of the Universe holds the plan. The plan of your present life was created from your past life, and the plan of your future life is now being drawn by your present life. When a man meets accident or sudden death, there is a reason for it.

'One such reason may interest you. In the past a man may have ended his life in a way that was not good. In the next life it may be his lot to pass out of the body suddenly through accident, because of that seed sown in the past. You will say that if all is in the plan, then man has no choice. Yes, man has choice. The choice is this – he can follow the guidance and the light of the highest self, and thus create beauty and goodness in his next life. Or he may react from the lowest aspect of himself and reap accordingly.'

A wise man once said that he had only to stand before someone's hearth and sense the vibrations therefrom to know intimately the family residing in that home. This was because those who lived in the home had imprinted their subtler selves on the etheric substance around that hearth for any sensitive person to read. We are all continually externalising ourselves in our homes, gardens, places of business, the neighbourhood where we live, and in our garments, to our friends, and everyone we meet. We externalise ourselves by our habits of speech and intonation, our choice of words, our appearance and condition of health. Our walk, gestures, mannerisms and facial expressions, all these are manifestations or externalisations of the inner man. An upright mind produces an upright man, straight of spine, with his solar plexus controlled. In the same way, a drooping, flabby mind is largely portrayed by the standing, sitting, walking, talking, thinking of its owner. Thus our very nature is making itself visible and audible in ways which are registered, not only by the physical senses of the beholder, but also by his subtler senses. We are attracted or repelled by someone at first sight because of what our subtler senses are telling us. So we live both in an outer and an inner world at one and the same time, the former seeming all important, the latter insignificant in comparison. Yet all the time we are busily externalising ourselves on both worlds, and that inner world is where we shall go after death.

For this inner world of the finer senses is present with us all the while, permeating this world as water does a sponge. We are affecting it, and it is in turn affecting us every moment of our lives, during which we are actively preparing the conditions to which we shall migrate after death, making ready our spirit home, as it were; furnishing it, planting flower seeds (or weed seeds) in its grounds – in other words, externalising ourselves on it. Have we ever longed for and been denied some home made wholly beautiful and serene? We can and shall some day realise that ideal home. Do we mourn the loss of some loved one who has gone before us, into apparent nothingness? That loved one has never been far distant, and can still come close to the inner heart. Only bitterness, resentment or just plain ignorance and lack of faith can shut out the companionship of that loved one; and love can still bridge any gulf, even that of death.

These points illustrate how closely the life beyond ties up with man's life here and now, and how unreasonable it is to separate them into compartments. We have to think about this earth as one of a series of such earths – ours being probably the darkest and coarsest of the series, in that its substance requires hard labour to alter or modify it, whereas the finer earths respond to and can be moulded by human thought and will power. Man is all the time (and unconsciously in the main) preparing his new home in the world beyond, where he can, God willing, store up treasure such as thieves cannot steal nor moth corrupt.

Man (declares the outer man) is primarily a body; and so to the outer man his bodily life is naturally his main interest and necessity. Man (says the inner man) is primarily spirit; and his body is only a garment worn by that spirit, discarded every night while he sleeps and finally cast off at death; and thus all other bodily things are just as unreal as the body itself. Closer to the spirit and so to reality are man's more intangible bodies such as the etheric and the astral, which are bodies of sensation and emotion: they record all the feelings and emotions to which they have responded during a lifetime – and that record is visible within their own substance, a substance more durable than physical matter because the higher etheric and astral bodies of man survive death, taking with them a complete record of an incarnation.

Thus when the soul comes into incarnation again it brings back the heritage left behind by its previous life – indeed, *the sins of the fathers are visited upon the children unto the third and fourth generation*, as the Bible has it, the generations of a soul being its incarnations. But not only the sins, by the way; good deeds are even more vital to the welfare of that soul because they are the more durable. Even if that descending soul is another aspect, another projection from its greater self, still must it take on itself its heritage from the past.

Where is all this line of thought leading us? Right away, surely, from the idea of our world being ruled by luck in any form, and towards the concept of a world of precise law and order – a law underlying and always rectifying apparent physical chaos. Another name for this precise law is the law of cause and effect, the law of karma, operative through all the ages of man and in all the worlds man will inherit and inhabit as he evolves.

There is something comforting in the thought of creation ruled by law. Our particular share of karma need not frighten us unless it be altogether bad; even then White Eagle says it can be transmuted by the power of love, and we can sow good karma to replace the bad. How should a man set about making good karma? He makes it by one means only – by reason of the love in his heart, which is his redeemer.

10

THE NEW MAN

You are here on earth to make use of physical matter, not to be dominated by it. You are essentially light and you have to shine out through the darkness. You have so to live that the light transmutes the heavy atoms of the physical body. Miracles happen when the spirit has gained such control.

W.E.

Let us turn once more to White Eagle:

'Man attains to spiritual or Christ consciousness through the lessons he is called upon to learn during his lives on earth, and principally through the practice of meditation on God, aspiration towards God. The evolving soul continually seeks to know more of the love of God and His wisdom; he learns to recognise and to depend on the strength of God. While God is above in the heavens, He is also beneath, in the very earth which sustains physical life. He is all around you, very close indeed to you externally; and He also dwells deep in your heart. This God within inspires your aspiration to rise, to search for the light, and, once found, to follow it without flinching or faltering. Keep your vision clear. Do not be deflected by the clamour and confusion of earth, nor by the disagreements between men. Keep strong in faith, and your faith will bring knowledge of all truth.

'We say again that the way to God is the way to happiness. God alone can give you strong and enduring happiness. While it is true that you will be confronted with many difficulties and trials in incarnation, remember also that everything you encounter will be something that you have attracted to yourself, for there is something in the soul which, like a magnet, draws to itself conditions which may bring sometimes pain and suffering, sometimes joy and peace. Your every thought, word and act are making their impression on the ether, and causing you to draw to your-self the very conditions which you yourself have formerly set in motion.

'But don't go about continually anticipating the worst! God doesn't call down pain and suffering on any of His children. He wants you to realise happiness and to glimpse the glory of the spirit. So we would bid you always expect the best, look for the best, but if anything comes along which you dislike, neverthe-less be thankful, knowing that you have drawn these things to yourself for a wise purpose. Your spirit is wiser than your mind, or even your soul. It has a deeper, clearer insight than has your earthly consciousness. Your soul is unwittingly crying out for light. The only way for it to obtain that light is by undergoing the experiences which it has attracted to itself.

'You have all known trial and tribulation; you have been tested on occasion to the last degree; and perhaps have watched your loved ones undergoing similar tests and trials and have been unable to help. Sometimes you have almost lost your faith in God. But after a while, when you are able to look back and see how perfect has been God's plan for you, you can say, "Thank God that things did not happen as I wanted them to happen! His way was far better than mine. How good is God!"

'The troubles and the inconveniences of the earthly life are unimportant, they are transient and will pass. Time is the great healer. No trouble lasts for ever, but your spiritual progress endures and is with you for eternity....'

A word about world happenings
'Don't fall into the habit of thinking that everything is getting worse, that all is lost; for you never made a bigger mistake! We can assure you that the world is making marked progress; the divine light is already penetrating the mists of confusion in man's mortal mind and reaching the hearts of men and women every-where. In the next few years you will see the spirit of man awakening; you will see greater interest in psychic and spiritual life. Things may not work out exactly as your mortal mind anticipates, but let us take the broad view, the long view. Behind

all seeming discord, greed and selfishness the spirit of God is ever active, bringing order out of chaos, good out of evil; bringing illumination to man. Don't look back with sadness; rather look forward with happy anticipation. . . .'

The new world

'We come back to the earth with a message of hope, of joy and reassurance that in the spirit of Christ, the Son of God, there is eternal life. This is eternal life, my brethren – the awakening of the soul to the love and beauty and wisdom of the Great White Spirit.

'Religion throughout the ages has given the same message, the message of the eternal life of the spirit, and the spirit is the Son of God. Jesus, who was a great channel for that light, said, *I am the way, the truth, and the life.* The I AM is the light of Christ in man. This is the message which the world of spirit is bringing you. The light of the world, the light of mankind, is the Christ spirit, which is within man's own heart. The great soul whom you call Jesus had been prepared through many incarnations to become a pure channel for that divine light, the Christ light. The Christ spirit is a universal spirit of love. Christ is love. And the life of Jesus of Nazareth demonstrated that love, demonstrated the gentleness and strength of the perfect Son of God.

'God is infinite, illimitable, God is all enfolding, God is within you and around you and above you and beneath you; you live and move and have your being in God. And the purpose of human life, the purpose of all your experiences, your striving, your sorrow, your joys, is to mould your spirit and soul into a perfect Son of God – man made perfect. This lies before every one of you, if you will remain loyal and true to the divine light in your heart.

'Man by his own striving and development of the power of the Son in his heart will change physical matter. You have the demonstration of this in the resurrection of Jesus, the Christ; and again, he said: *He that believeth on me, the works that I do shall he do also.* With this growth of the Christ light in physical matter there will be a purification and a beautifying of all life, until this planet, this dark star, becomes a brilliant sun – not tomorrow, but in the eternal life.'

With these words our search for the cause of illness concludes. It does not, however, follow that having found the cause we have of necessity found the universal cure. *Seek and ye shall find*, we are told. Some there are who can be healed, as it were instantaneously and apparently magically. The days of miracles are not past; not that there is in fact anything magical about such healings – they follow a natural law, and everything depends on the soul's degree of spiritual awareness, of spiritual evolution. At a certain stage such a healing is like putting a match to a long-prepared torch. Everything becomes illumined, so that the enraptured soul sees God face to face, and thus seeing becomes suddenly and miraculously healed.

This by its very nature can seldom happen. It is likely that many may well be wanting healing, but will be held back by grave doubts of their ability to overrule body and head minds. These doubts, they will find, are not without foundation, for the body mind offers a dour resistance and the head mind is always rushing in, with its disconnected and often futile thoughts, to overwhelm the poor heart mind whenever it attempts to pray or meditate. The average person has indeed a long and stern fight before him before he can regain rule over body and head minds.

We come now to a curative method which is so simple, so natural, so easy for the average man to practise, and so promising in its results, that folk will some day turn to it for healing almost instinctively.

It is born of a new outlook on life, a new mode of living, and the acceptance of life as something to be valued and served with an eager heart. To call White Eagle's philosophy for living a religion would perhaps deter some people, who may fail to recognise that all of it can be found within the framework of the Christianity given by Jesus, although here some of it is implied rather than expressed.

Does the philosophy of living unfolded by White Eagle work? Has it stood by people when they are bereaved, or find themselves in deep trouble and anxiety? Does it answer the searching of the heart? Has it power to heal more than the body of man? Yes, indeed. Over the years it has been tested and not found wanting. It has justified itself as a real and hard-wearing philosophy of life. Readers should bear this factor in mind; for while it is good to heal bodies, it is far greater to bring peace into a tormented life. True healing is arrived at through the healing of the soul. A spiritual healer is also a spiritual teacher, and the spiritual light which emanates from him is the healing light.

Part II

A New Healing – The Training of a Healer – How to Heal Others

11

A CENTURY OF USEFUL LIVING

Look beneath the outer mask of your everyday life. Look beneath the outer mask of words. Seek the true spirit.

W.E.

Some of us have settled by now, it is to be hoped, that henceforth it will be our modest aim to reach a century of useful living! Experts agree that the average man should live to at least this age, the basis of their reasoning being the extensive period that infant man takes to grow to maturity, in common with any other species of long-living animals. Given the will to do so, a century should therefore be attainable, always providing that *homo sapiens* does not wilfully cut himself off from his power house, from his Creator; given also that he masters the self-destructive element in himself which would drag him down to premature age and death.

Let no one think that such a mastery will be easy to achieve. Yet so precious a treasure is worth prolonged effort, worth an eventual surrender of the hard outer self. Who shall be faithful all the way? Not everyone; for with the best will in the world, not everybody can remain steadfastly on the path. The purpose of the second part of this book is therefore to help the wayfarer on his journey. Since the cause of disease is primarily spiritual, the cure must essentially be spiritual also; but because most of us have to live in a largely material and insensitive world, most of us will require additional help.

The method of healing now to be described is not to be re-garded as an easy cure for everything; and any curative method should always be regarded as supplementary or complementary to the healing of the self by the deeper self. No true healing of soul or body can take place without some corresponding spiritual effort on the part of the patient, but the patient can be helped, his own efforts supplemented; his spirit can be nurtured and strengthened.

For a moment, let us look back. What have we learnt, so far? The root cause of illness has been sought, and one method of cure indicated. So far so good; but also it has been hinted that perhaps it is not always right or good for the sufferer to be healed immediately. Illness may have much to teach in the way of humility, patience, and self-discipline. But the sufferer can be vastly helped if he has some inkling of what his illness comes to teach. He needs a philosophy of life which makes being ill bearable. Nothing will ever seem rational to those who know not where they are going or, indeed, if they are going anywhere.

Spiritual healing, the White Eagle method of healing, is wholly natural, not dependent on drugs or any other recognised form of therapy. So natural is it that it might almost be described as spontaneous, as when a mother runs to pick up her crying baby after a tumble, and rubs and kisses the place to make it well. She is then instinctively putting the method into practice. In the same way, when we suffer a blow on the head, or a bang on the shin, we instinctively try to rub the pain away with our hand. We don't bother to reason this out – all we know is that by rubbing, the pain will lessen or disappear. So also when we painstakingly rub so-and-so's wonderful liniment or embrocation into strains or sprains, we ascribe any resulting benefit to the embrocation rather than to the rubbing. It is a matter for everyday demonstration that the human hand can rub or stroke pain away. In other words, any reasonably healthy person can transfer some of his surplus health to a sick person, and by so doing relieve local pain or discomfort.

An illustration of this faculty can be found in the practice of 'palming', which is one of a series of exercises designed to strengthen and restore failing eyesight and obviate the use of glasses. Having done his exercises, the student of eyecraft rests his eyes in the palms of his hands, and remains thus resting for some minutes. Could it be that this palming proves so effective, because the healing power of the hands is thus transferred to the weakened eyes?

Another illustration is taken from a cutting from a Sunday newspaper. It tells how a woman in an old people's home collapsed and died after a heart attack. Her heart and pulse stopped beating. When the matron started to lay the body out, she thought, as she moved the dead hands, that she detected the faintest flicker of life. Then it was gone. She started to massage the dead heart, even though she was sure the patient was dead and could not be revived. She kept moving her hands in a circular direction round the heart and back. Perspiration poured from her. For sixteen minutes there was no beat from the heart. The woman was to all intents and purposes dead. But as the matron's experienced hands kept up their sweeping circular passes, life began slowly to return. The heart beat quickened. The patient had cheated death. Her first whispered words were, 'Where have I been? I have been away from here.'

The matron was asked how she herself felt after such an experience. She answered that she was trembling. Afterwards she almost collapsed. The patient, however, the oldest woman in the home, was bubbling with life.

This dramatic little story should interest spiritual healers, who will be familiar with the whole procedure, including the feeling of exhaustion after some mighty effort.

This transferring of power from one to another is an elementary form of healing and has been recognised down the ages. It is what is known as magnetic healing, the pouring in of magnetism from healer to patient.

Anyone can put this to the test by trying to relieve someone's headache, earache, backache or other pain by a gentle touch of the hand or by stroking or rubbing. This form of magnetic healing does not necessarily effect a permanent cure – it is a means of alleviation, an easing of discomfort. It is natural healing at its simplest – no more than this. True spiritual healing, rightly understood and practised, is a very different matter, and is permanent in its effect. It will not be found to be unduly dependent on what is commonly called faith – faith in this sense being taken as an earnest effort on the part of somebody to believe something he simply can't believe. True faith – which is indeed necessary for true spiritual healing – is knowledge put into practice; that is, knowledge of God being lived out in the life. Faith expresses this inner knowing.

So far, so good; we begin with the most common form of healing – magnetic healing, or the transfer of surplus strength or health from one person to another (how often mothers could help their sick child in this way and how natural and right this help would be!).

Now, to assist and prepare the healer for his ministry of healing; and it will presently be seen how simple (and how arduous) such a preparation is likely to be.

We human beings are indeed fearfully and wonderfully made. None can deny that man's fleshly body is a miraculous conception miraculously wrought. Were it only as perfect as God conceived it and as it can become, the perfect man would be the triumph of God and the wonder of the universe.

But to understand how magnetic healing, and indeed spiritual healing generally, operates it must be realised, as said, that man possesses other and more refined bodies than the coarser physical. These several bodies interpenetrate and infuse the latter, and are successively brighter and more beautiful; each body will in turn become man's main habitation as he himself grows brighter and more beautiful in spirit.

Each body in its degree animates the physical. Drive out those bodies for the time being, say by a blow on the head, or by an anaesthetic, and the man lies unconscious. Man has, it is said, seven bodies in all, corresponding to the seven planes of existence which will await him after death, and each has its own particular aura.

The etheric body is that unrealised body so close to the physical that it is not wholly invisible or intangible. Without it, man would have no sense of touch or hearing, taste or smell, no sight. His body is saturated by the etheric as a soaked sponge is saturated by water or air fills a feather bed; and its emanation or auric surround extends for several inches beyond the physical. This etheric body serves as a bridge during mortal life over which the life force reaches the physical body; only the grosser portion disintegrates after the death of the physical body, and the finer portion lives on and forms part of the equipment of the newly reincarnating soul.

We are encased by our etheric aura, very much as the human skin encloses and protects the delicate flesh beneath it. It largely fulfils the same purpose of protection, being itself a kind of skin, which protects not so much against the blows incidental to physical existence, but against attacks from the thought world, for in that thought world may reside some undesirable entities – and these entities can obtain entry through a damaged aura, sometimes resulting in obsession and insanity.

These things are mentioned only in passing, but may help to make clear one of the purposes served by the aura as an indispensable part of man's make-up. More than this, the aura provides a means for diagnosing complaints, since the bodily and mental conditions govern its entire colour scheme. A person abounding in health and well-being has an aura of a bright clear hue. He is quite literally in the pink. Should he later become depressed and ill, his aura takes on a murky grey-blue – he has the blues. Sudden anger suffuses the aura with darting flames – the man is then seeing red. Jealousy, an ugly thing, is reflected by the aura as a dirty green – the man is green with envy. These sayings suggest that man already unconsciously possesses some knowledge concerning the aura.

White Eagle says: 'Man has three lower bodies, physical, etheric, astral and each has its aura. The clairvoyant, according to his or her degree of development, may see one or other of these auras. Beyond the bodily aura are the auras emanating from the emotional, the intellectual, the intuitional bodies. And then beyond again, probably outside the range of most clairvoyant vision, wait the glorious auras of the celestial body, of the human spirit or individuality; of the light, life or Christ consciousness; and of the divine consciousness, or at-one-ment with God.

'When you grow tired it is because you have failed to plug into the power station. You may be sceptical about this, but it is true – if, through aspiration, through love and harmony you plug into the power station of the Christ light, you will receive an unending flow of the vital life force into your being and you will know neither weariness nor frustration.

'Now do you see how the pure healing from the Christ sphere, the light shining down through the various bodies of man, can restore the whole being to perfect health?'

This teaching on auras is not altogether outside the business of daily life, because most of us are affected by the auras of others, which can expand to enfold our own on occasions. This is how an orator can grip and hold his listeners, or an actor keep his audience spellbound. As a contrast, the aura of some drunkard may infect us with fumes of alcohol. It is said that certain diseases can be transmitted to others via the physical aura. Against this the aura of someone good and strong has power to infuse us with a good courage, not always dependent on what is said, but on the feeling conveyed, as one aura impinges on another. For instance, if you were to touch the aura of a master, which can extend a great distance, you would receive a wonderful enlightenment and purification. This brings home to us our own responsibility to ensure that the brightness of our own aura may help and inspire rather than depress others.

Let us suppose that we ourselves (possessing no more knowledge than is ours at the moment) were suddenly called on to give a healing treatment. How shall we tackle the job?

Our patient's aura is drooping and drab. Our own, let us hope, is vibrant and clear. We are about to go to work, primarily on our patient's etheric body, with our own etheric body. We are going to clear and cleanse his aura of its greyness and shadows. We shall do this by passing our hands again and again through the aura, thereby in effect combing out that greyness. We shall make passes from our patient's head to his feet. We shall comb the aura of the whole body. Again and again we comb through that aura, putting all our spiritual will power into the effort. Having completed the treatment we shall find that the patient already looks better. He seems nearly asleep. We steal away. After a while he comes out looking considerably lighter, brighter, more cheerful, saying that most of the pain has left him, and goes on his way rejoicing. What has happened? Only that his aura has been cleansed by the passes we have made; that its greyness (semi-material stuff) has been combed out, and that the little particles of pain have gone away with it.

Simple and reasonable enough, do you not think? And, as has been said, readily put to the test. As for the greyness being semi-material, let the healer examine his hands, which will feel sticky and dirty, so that when he washes his hands afterwards the water will be tinged.

Don't let anyone think that the whole process of healing has been covered in this one imaginary healing treatment. All that has been done is to clear the aura of accumulated greyness and diseased matter; pain has been removed but the greyness and pain will doubtless recur – until the *cause* of this accumulation has been healed. We have yet to learn the first essential. This lies, not in the auras and their combing out, nor yet in any physical or semi-physical substance, but deep within the spiritual quality of the healer. Therein lies the key.

12

THE WISDOM HEALING

While all souls have to work in accordance with the law, each soul is entirely individual. This will give you some insight into the meaning of the Master's words when he said, but even the very hairs of your head are all numbered. From the waster in the gutter to the wisest in the land, every soul remains attuned in its degree to the Divine Intelligence, and must ultimately follow the one pathway which will lead it back to God.

THE RETURN OF ARTHUR CONAN DOYLE

White Eagle continues: 'A few words about the power of thought. Thought can create good health, thought can also heal; and thought can inflict pain and disease; it can disrupt and destroy the bodily, mental and soul life of man. Thoughts of anger, fear and hate form the root of all suffering and of wars. Thought can also bring beauty, harmony, and brotherhood and all else for which man longs. We ourselves work always on the principle of the creative power of thought; we try to avoid all destructive thought. We make it a rule when giving advice and help always to construct, to see nothing but good. We know that we may be called foolishly optimistic, but we know also that by seeing only good, by creating good by positive thought, we can help to bring about that which is desirable and good. Never see or think in terms of pessimism, sadness or death. All is life, all is unfolding, all is ever progressing – all is good, all is God.

'Would-be healers should always work constructively. Admit no such thing as death. See only creation – ever-changing, ever-unfolding life. Never anticipate anything but good; believe that while there is life there is hope. It is the work of all true healers to inspire confidence; always help the patient to attune him or herself harmoniously to the divine laws of God.'

It would seem that thought can create or destroy us. We can be self-redemptive, self-creative; or we can become so self-destructive in our thoughts that even while we continue to exist we are yet only half alive. But the word thought hardly conveys all that is wanted, because it limits us to the activities of the head mind, whereas the body mind does some thinking for itself, in an automatic sort of way; while the heart mind, silent, watchful, remote and self-effacing, is ever the true, *feeling* self within us. Feeling is a close neighbour to thinking – in fact, it might be said that what the head mind wants to do, the heart mind hastens to put into practice; that while the head mind is busy thinking, the heart mind is being.

Therefore the most potent cure for any complaint is the heart-felt will to get well, a will reinforced and put into effect by every power of man's body, mind and spirit.

What has been said about the power of thought, about the will to health, about man's largely unused capacity for regenerating himself and thereby living to a healthy, happy, active and useful old age, at the end of which he finds death kindly and gracious, applies not only to the patient (who must be helped to co-operate in his healing by the healer encouraging this will to get well) but even more forcibly to the healer; for indeed a man or woman does not become a healer until some measure of self-mastery has been acquired as a first step. This brings us back again to White Eagle, who makes it plain that the healer must be simple and humble of spirit, hard working and very patient. He says:

Self-purification
'The first step, then, for the would-be healer is that of self-purification. You may have the desire to heal others, but if the pure mountain water – the divine healing spirit – has to pass through a muddied channel, it must lose its properties, its qualities of healing. This purification of the healer may seem slow, but it can be quickened. Do not, please, feel despondent about this first step, because you can still be used according to your potential, at

first in lesser and then in greater degree. Since your heart is laid upon the altar of service, you will be anxious and willing to do all in your power to make ready. Love and willingness are valuable attributes in any healer, but we need more – we need the development of the will, both the steadfast will to serve, and the strong and developed will power to concentrate the healing rays, which you will be taught how to contact and direct.

'One of the commonest causes of inharmony is strain. So many people make the mistake of overreaching themselves, of overstraining, of trying to cram too much into a day and of going to bed too late in consequence. You will protest your innocence, asking what you are to do about it, seeing that there is so much to be done. We answer that you all work far too hard *in your minds*; that is to say, you are apt to do your work in your minds a hundred times before you actually tackle it. It is well for healers to try to control this busy and wayward head mind; to cultivate the habit of tranquillity, of placidity of temperament, for you will want to convey these qualities to your patient, who will often come to you emotionally storm driven, like a boat on a rough sea, and you will have first to help him to find peace and a measure of self control.

'All healing consists of the restoration of peace to the soul of the patient. And remember every soul restored makes a contribution to the healing of the whole world. All the world needs healing, needs peace; and we suggest that you say to yourselves, inwardly many times a day *Peace, be still*. Let the Christ within you answer: *I am within you. I am divine peace . . . divine peace. . . .* This will help you to become more peaceful, to become still within.

'The greatest healer ever known is Jesus the Christ, and all healers must be his disciples, for from the Christ centre, the Son in man, all healing flows. Jesus the Great Healer is at the head of the sixth ray, the ray of spiritual science, and healing is essentially a spiritual science. Even Jesus at times required certain conditions to be fulfilled in order to perform his healing miracles. For instance, you will remember how, when he approached Jairus' daughter who was through to be dead, and there was a great

noise of wailing and weeping around the little girl, Jesus first
cleared the room except for a chosen few. Then, when all was
still, he restored the little one to life. This will indicate that the
better the conditions you can create for healing, the better results
will you get. This is why we always tell our healers how necessary
it is to preserve silence during healing, because silence both creates
and conserves the healing power. . . .'

Ever deeper understanding
'When you are healing you will soon become aware that your
patient's disease represents some lack of ease which began not in
the body but in the soul. The particular dis-ease to be treated is
sometimes the result of quite recent karma. In a sense, of course,
all disease is karmic, because everything must result from a cause;
but if that cause reaches back to a former incarnation the disease
is deep rooted and is the outworking of some needed lesson. More
general are cases where karma has been set in motion during a
present incarnation, operating in the course of hours, days, weeks
or months. There is always a cause behind any sickness. Sometimes
that cause is rooted in ignorance, sometimes in waywardness, as
when a patient deliberately persists in doing something which he
knows perfectly well is unwise – such as, for instance, eating food
which he knows will disagree with him. He eats it and gets
indigestion. He knows perhaps that certain other habits of his are
not in accordance with divine and natural law, yet he persists in
them, and eventually his body rebels. Your own experience can
tell you how quickly karma will sometimes overtake the sinner.
   'In spiritual healing don't concentrate too much on physical
symptoms. Don't be too concerned with the physical aspect of
the case at all, for you are dealing primarily with the patient's soul
and aura. We have also noticed healers being a little too pressing
in their treatment. Don't work too hard *of yourself.* Your real task
is to make contact with a higher plane of being, and to offer
yourself as the bridge across which subtle spiritual forces can flow.
Often you need barely touch the sick body. Do it gently, very
lightly. What you will most need is to keep constant contact,
shall we say, with your master, or with the healing brotherhood.

Focus your heart and mind on the invisible brotherhood of helpers and the light which comes from them. Steadfastly maintain contact with that centre of healing and, having done so, conceive perfection in the patient. Then you must convey that thought of perfection to your patient, not by words so much as by the power of your spirit; and by this means give him confidence. You can only make this true spiritual contact in silence.

'. . . Of course, karma does not always manifest in the form of physical illness, but can come out in the harassing circumstances and material difficulties which beset a life. A wise healer will know that he cannot interfere here; although we must qualify this by saying that the healer should in time acquire a sensitivity which will enable him to sense the soul or psychological trouble of his patient, and help that patient to see aright. For good can overcome evil, love overcome hate, light disperse darkness. Through the power of the Christ love in its own heart the soul can win through to redemption, and release itself from the bondage of its own karma. Once you can make the true spiritual contact and help patients to release themselves from soul troubles, you are indeed well on the road to becoming a good healer.'

The wisdom healing
'In ancient days the practice of healing was always confined to the temples and was thought of purely as a spiritual service, although herbs were used and certain juices of plants were made into ointments and lotions. Music and colour also formed part of the healing. Nevertheless, all healing was confined to the temple service. Medical science today has become divorced from religious belief and has become largely a science of the physical body. However, it is beginning to recognise the spiritual or soul causation of disease, and in days to come the medical student will study spiritual law in order to obtain a clear picture of his patient's soul records. While both medicine and surgery do some very wonderful things, in some respects they are unable to deal with the real ills of mankind. So always remember in your healing that you must concentrate on the spiritual aspect; you must not be drawn

to the material aspect and then waver between the two. In constancy and confidence shall be your strength.

'Every healer must learn to face his own problems and learn from his own mistakes. Nevertheless a call sent out from you to the unseen helpers will always be answered, although the answer may not come in the way you expect or hope. Try, however, as a good healer, to become impervious to apparent failures by remaining very sure that spiritual power is always ultimately effective. But as a rule it has to work through the soul first before lasting bodily improvement can take place. A soul bound by its past debts may be slow in response. The healer must be humble enough to accept apparent failure, and to keep on keeping on, unmoved by failure or success. Be philosophical about the former; be humble about the latter. Possibly even Jesus did not heal everyone who came to him. . . .'

Talk about purity may come as rather a deterrent to some would-be healers. We have in mind a certain fellow worker who prided himself on his strength and fitness, which he was convinced resulted from his hearty appetite for all the enjoyable things of life. This man enjoyed healing the sick by transferring some of his surplus vitality to them. He was an admirable and lovable fellow. All honour to him in his service to his fellows. But in the end he had to give up his healing because he lacked that particular toughness and resilience which carries a spiritual healer along. Perhaps another healer's report on a specially difficult case will help us to understand what is meant here. The report reads:

'As requested, I write out this account of a recent healing experience. My patient was from Australia, a huge fellow weighing perhaps twenty stone, who looked the typical tough guy of the films, except that he felt very sick and sorry for himself. Nobody, he said, could do him any good. He had a mind, I should say, which could deal only with the obvious things of life, and when anything outside these came along he was out of his depth. One had to adjust one's conversation accordingly so that he could understand. Another difficulty was that his way of speaking and mine were partially unintelligible one to the other.

'I took him into the chapel. He seemed rather wary and

on the defensive. He would have smoked in the chapel if I had not checked him. I gathered from him afterwards that he had not been in a church before. Obviously he knew nothing of spiritual healing. His huge form dwarfed the chapel, and I felt rather like a mouse about to give a healing treatment to a mountain. I sat him down in a chair and little by little extracted his sad and rather grim story. He had recently lost his wife, who had died of cancer. Some weeks before her passing she had been taken to a giant hospital. Within these walls his wife had died, but not for several weeks, during which time he had seen and heard things which he could never forget, sights and sounds which haunted him now. He had come on this trip to try to shake them off, but he couldn't. He had chronic backache which he was told was due to kidney trouble. To combat this his doctor had prescribed drugs, which hadn't done any good. He also had dreadful constipation, and was taking drugs for that. But nothing had helped much there either. He was now in constant pain, and felt he was going mad. He didn't know what all this was about (meaning the chapel and my white-coated presence) but he was getting desperate and would try anything.

'By this time I was beginning to understand his case a little. When one has healed for many years the sense of touch soon enables one to locate the trouble. It didn't seem to be in his back. I touched his poor sore head, which he said was always aching. That head had good cause to ache. I judged his trouble to be delayed shock, or an incipient nervous breakdown, brought about by the happenings in that hospital, and his very real and tragic grief at his wife's passing. I treated him for shock and nervous exhaustion. When the treatment was over, and he was lying relaxed on the bed, he asked me (he was nearly asleep) when I was going to do something for him. I said I had already done what I wanted to do – that he had had his healing treatment.

'Half an hour later I collected him, still very drowsy. He promised me that he would obtain a tin of crude black molasses, and take a large dose daily of this food for his constipation, and yeast tablets to help his nervous exhaustion.

'I wondered whether he would ever keep his appointment with

me for a week later. I thought that it was likely however, because I felt that I had a grip on his complaint and could master it, given time. Make no mistake – my grip was only on his complaint, I had no sort of hypnotic link over the man himself. Healing is just not done that way. But one has to feel able to master a disease before it can be healed.

'Sure enough, he came back. What a change there was in him! He reminded me of nothing so much as an abashed and elated schoolboy. He was receptive now, where he had been bumptious before, and very ready indeed to listen. This chastened frame of mind was because he felt so much better. He didn't know what had happened, or why it had happened, he just felt better all over, and couldn't contain his surprise.

'This was my opportunity for a little straight talking. Also he was handed some leaflets about diet and physical well-being. He went away with a book of White Eagle's teaching. Whether or not he could understand it is another matter. He sailed two days later.'

This account was written by a practised spiritual healer who has disciplined his life to the service of healing. The reader will decide whether the first healer (who had never had a day's illness) would have been the man to handle this patient, or whether the man who actually coped with him was the more suitable. It could be argued, however, that in the spiritual sense the first is not a healer at all, but a disperser of bodily symptoms. Powers such as this are very valuable on occasion. But they are not the be all and end all of spiritual healing, which is essentially a soul as well as a bodily healing of the patient, the soul healing usually preceding any body healing. This is why White Eagle has so stressed the necessity for purity on the healer's part.

13

SAY RATHER, 'HERE AM I, LORD; SEND ME'

*When one reviews life and examines closely the long experience
which is inevitable before man draws near to spiritual completion, one recognises not only the necessity for reincarnation,
but the tremendous importance of every detail of life.*

THE RETURN OF ARTHUR CONAN DOYLE

If anyone wants to demonstrate spiritual healing on himself, let
him wait his opportunity. What the writer has in mind is one of
those agonising bumps on the head or bangs on the shin, or a
twisted ankle, a nasty fall, or any painful occurrence of this
nature, to which we are all occasional victims. Then is the time
to put self-healing to the test. Let the victim with all his might
declare that he is spirit therefore no pain nor any injury can
touch him that cannot be immediately dispersed by the power of
divine love. Let him call upon the light, draw the light into his
being, and sure enough his pain will lessen or disappear. To try
out this method is to prove it; and even if the injury prove severe,
by continuing his aspiration the trouble will depart far more
speedily than if its victim becomes cowed and yields to pain.
There is no ill that cannot respond to the power of the spirit in
man, if he knows how to use it. There is indeed much for man to
learn about himself and his capacity for self-regeneration.

The etheric hands of the healer play an important part in all
healing, for the physical body of the patient presents no barrier
to them. They can penetrate into the body; they can reach any
complaint, however deep seated. The site of that complaint will
take shape as a dark patch in the etheric body of the patient. The
etheric hands of the healer can by degrees loosen that patch and
disperse it by passes through the aura. As already said, the aura of

a healthy person, when seen by a clairvoyant, is bright, vigorous, with all its colours clear and brilliant; the aura of a sick man is drooping, dull, and interspersed with grey substance, more especially at the seat of the complaint. By passes, by combing out the aura, as it is called, this greyness, which is the cause of much pain, can be cleared. When watching this clearing, a clairvoyant would see the grey substance being drawn out through the aura by the hands of the healer.

It should be realised that in magnetic healing we are still manipulating matter, albeit in a less tangible form. We are still dealing with bodily things, although appertaining to a finer body than the gross physical.

The healer should always discriminate between alleviating symptoms and effecting an actual cure. To cure means to go to the root of things. To dispel pain is not enough. That pain is a warning of some deeper disharmony within, probably aggravated by wrong feeding, wrong habits of life and of thought. The one essential in healing is contact with the spirit. All else is subsidiary. The true spiritual healing takes place when that spirit can so pour through the healer as to quicken the soul of the patient.

The priest healer in ancient Egypt, by the touch of merciful hands, healed sickness, wounds and injuries which today might take weeks or months to treat. At the same time he healed the soul of the sufferer, for these people were deeply versed in ancient wisdom.

White Eagle says: 'We look far, far back into the history of mankind and we see this same Christ healing being practised through the ages, in civilisations now gone. The healing light has always existed, and it was always the chosen priests and priestesses who were called to their particular mission to become instruments through whom this healing power was transmitted to the sick. So very little is known today about the age-old art of spiritual healing. We don't deny the progress of medical science. The surgeon can carry out wonderful operations on the body of man when, probably through man's own ignorance or neglect, an operation becomes necessary; or after an accident when surgery will often be the only available method of repairing the damage.

'But in the coming era wisdom as well as knowledge will be given again to man; there will be concentration on the prevention of illness rather than on the cure of complaints that should never have arisen. People will learn to treat their bodies with consideration and care. It is not egotistical to take good care of your body. It is the duty of every child of God. Whenever we see misuse of the beautiful human instrument which God has created with such love, it makes us very sad. The abuse and misuse of man's body is mainly due to his ignorance. As he becomes more enlightened and grows spiritually he will refrain from punishing himself in this way. This is where spiritual illumination is so vitally necessary; for as people evolve spiritually, in the degree that they receive illumination both from within and from without they will realise the importance of the laws governing all life. They will recognise that it is wrong to abuse the body by overstrain, by overeating, and impure feeding, by indulgence in bad habits, and by wrong thinking.

'Often the soul incarnates in a body that is prone to disease because for karmic reasons it has chosen to follow that particular path. It recognises that it will only learn what is necessary through suffering; it is reaping the harvest of seeds already sown. But by your healing power you can help your patient to open his eyes to truth, and thus to transmute his karma. Karma is a cosmic law, but this does not necessarily mean that healing cannot take place because of a man's karma, for the healer can help the patient to dissolve his karma. Maybe the karma is deep and it may take a long time for it to be eradicated, or for the debts to be paid. But this we can assure you, that the actual service of healing can never fail.

'All karma will eventually work out, and then there will no longer be any necessity for the soul to incarnate in a weak body, prone to pain. So it is very important for healers not only to take account of these laws in their own lives, but to try gently to spread knowledge regarding the right care of the physical body....'

Recognising a saint
'A quality by which you will recognise a true healer is humility. We are thinking of the saints, and particularly of St. Francis of

Assisi, who was so imbued with the Christ spirit and the light that he radiated healing, as did Jesus. Jesus did not even have to touch the person, he could heal at a distance, and even to touch the hem of his garment was to be healed. To lay a healing hand on a fevered brow, to take away pain, to comfort the brokenhearted and the troubled in spirit, is a very beautiful and wonderful gift. This gift comes to the man or woman who has something of the quality of consciousness of a saint.

'Now, do not say, even to yourselves, "Then I shall never be a healer." Leave it in God's hands. Say rather, "Here am I, Lord; use me if you will. You alone know what you have implanted in me. If it be your will, use that power to your honour and glory and for the healing of souls." That is the right attitude towards your work of healing. We ourselves are nothing; God is everything. All the same, you can seek certain attributes which will help in the making of the true healer. The first of these is simplicity, true humility and purity.

'Jesus said ... *many are called, but few are chosen.* This is true. There are many who wish to become healers, who believe they are called to the mission of healing; but there are only comparatively few who are instruments born to exercise it. This is what we should like all of you to be able to do.

'First of all came love for God. Jesus was continually speaking about His Father. This applies to you, today. First in your heart must come God, your contact with God. First and foremost man lives to serve all life. He serves best by living to worship God. Again: ... *thou shalt love the Lord thy God with all thy heart, and with all thy soul, and with all thy mind, and with all thy strength ... Thou shalt love thy neighbour as thyself.* Jesus did not say we should love our neighbour *more* than ourselves, but that we should love our neighbour *as* ourselves. This surely means that one should love oneself; love one's body, take care of it, treat it kindly, considerately, reverently. In the degree that you love and serve your neighbour, love yourself also. This is not selfish, for by this means you are equipping yourself for God's service, making yourself a better instrument. But the very first thing is to love God.

'You must remember that all healing power flows from God; and in the degree you are close to God (as the saints have always been close to God) He will give you the sweet healing power which can touch even the heart of sorrow.

'You are learning to become a bridge between this world of darkness and the world of light. Wherever you go, whoever you meet, remember that you are a bridge across which the angels can travel, bringing light and healing to the earth life. Is it not a comforting thought? Does it not make your life worth while, wherever you are, however humble you are? Indeed we are going to say that the more humble and gentle and loving the man or woman, the purer is the channel, the better the bridge.

'Jesus, the Great Healer, the master of all healing on this earth, is older than this earth planet, and he has always been a healer. There have been many teachers on the earth, who have come in different bodies into different nationalities, to different civilisations, but behind all these manifestations, no matter what the nationality or the civilisation, there has always been the Teacher Healer. Those two go together because the teacher brings simple wisdom. Every patient needs teaching, otherwise they would not need healing. If a man understands truth he has found peace, and he does not know any lack of ease or disease. He is whole, perfectly whole. Every healer, or channel for the Great Healer, must learn to be wise and extremely humble and gentle and loving. Rough words, harsh words, condemnation, judgment? Never. The teacher healer never judges, never condemns, only helps his patient to his feet, and is gentle and loving; but behind that gentleness, which can be likened to the velvet glove, is a firm grip, a mind that is positive. The healer must have a velvet glove over a strong hand; and the touch on the patient, the word to the patient, must always be clothed in gentleness and loving kindness. This was the way that your Master, the Great Healer always worked, and, through you, can still work.'

14

THE PURE LIFE

In the days to come a new humanity will arise. Men will begin to search their hearts and will listen to the voice of conscience which will tell them that it is a great sin to be cruel in thought or deed, and especially to the helpless. . . . In fifty years' time men will no longer eat the flesh of their brothers the animals. They will regard this practice with repugnance. . . . Already you can see indications of this change of heart coming.

W.E.

Let it be clear that this chapter is addressed to those people whose interest in healing is deep and sincere; to those who will consider no sacrifice too great, who would be willing to surrender any dearly held and indulged habit if to forego it would make them a better healer; and to those who already realise that the supremely important factor in healing is the spiritual quality of the healer; that it is what a man *is* rather than what he *does* for a patient which decides the cure.

All of us possess habits so deeply ingrained that we never think of them as other than normal and natural. Because we have always done this or that, or thought thus about certain things, or eaten certain foods cooked in a certain way, we expect to continue on these lines – as our parents did before us, so we carry on. Ingrained habits have become a part of us, and we regard any suggestion of change with impatience and incredulity.

Yet White Eagle tells us that before this century is out a revolution in man's thinking will have come about – that man will regard the very idea of eating the flesh of brother animal with very much the same aversion as the eating of human flesh would arouse today. Apart from economic and health reasons, he will recoil from the cruelty involved.

Animals taken to slaughter are forced into pens and places reeking with the smell of blood and death. They often linger in such conditions before they are killed, so that when death comes their whole bodies, physical and etheric, are saturated with fear. Later, when the carcases are distributed as butcher's meat and consumed, those who eat it in turn assimilate that fear into themselves, and this process is happening daily – often several times a day. It is true that cattle, sheep and pigs do not outwardly display the same alarm, and would appear phlegmatic. Notwithstanding this, can it be reasonably argued that living, sensitive creatures such as these do not know that death is approaching and have no apprehension about it?

Consider also the fearsome psychic conditions which afflict places set apart for the slaughter of animals. A slaughterhouse sends out a psychic infection or contamination which affects a wide area around it; as an example, people who have lived in Buenos Aires speak of the dreadful psychic and moral emanations from the great slaughter factories which dominate that town. Even the physical conditions are bad enough, they say, when the wind blows towards the city from the abattoirs. But there is always a kind of moral contamination coming from those places where animals are killed in countless numbers.

An eye for an eye; a tooth for a tooth, decreed the Jewish law. Jesus Christ came to repeal that law, but only for those who become men of Christ. Otherwise the law stands, and worldly man must forfeit an eye for an eye and a tooth for a tooth. *Be not deceived;* said Paul, *God is not mocked: for whatsoever a man soweth, that shall he also reap.* The blood of the innocent, we are told in several places in the Bible, cries out to heaven. These sayings are a statement of how the law of karma will work out. Together with these must be set yet another saying, this time by White Eagle, who at the time was voicing a truth uttered by another of the sages. This was to the effect that as surely as man sheds the blood of the animal kingdom, so must he in turn be prepared to shed his own blood; for this also is how the law works; this is karma. None can dispute or withstand this law, for it is justice in action; and it applies not only to those who actually shed the blood of animals but to those who breed animals for slaughter, and to all who consume the flesh of animals (and how unthinkingly!).

Some truths may of necessity seem unpalatable. The pity of it is that they should still need repeating after two thousand years of Christianity. They can be denied, of course. They will be denied. Yet while he denies, man is continually shedding his own blood. People are injured or die by violence in their thousands on the roads or in accidents of various kinds. Violence begets violence, and all slaying is violence, and its acme is war, as this generation so sadly knows.

A century or two ago, this was a country largely subsisting on beef and beer. Since then food habits have been modified, so that year by year salads, fresh fruits and wholefoods have become more popular. Possibly because of this, new humanities arise. The span of life of man increases, partly because greater care is taken of the race in infancy, and partly because instead of being largely a physical creature man's mental and spiritual nature is evolving. He is therefore acquiring a body of finer material which has a greater hold on life. The gross feeding of a century ago tended to shorten lives.

Claim and disclaim, argument and rejoinder, can endlessly revolve around this subject. There are those who will advance the case of some man who lived perhaps for a century by means of indulging in everything harmful to his body – by eating huge quantities of unsuitable foods, by drinking largely, smoking copiously, and so forth – as a conclusive argument; regardless of the fact that exceptions to a rule prove nothing, except that here was someone so naturally a gross eater that he flourished on it. In any case, argument settles nothing and may evade the issue. There are those to whom the thought of eating the flesh of an animal is abhorrent, and those who believe that it is natural and right to do so. The latter never think about the animals' feelings in the matter, for flesh of animals is to them something they buy in a shop. They constitute a majority of the race at the present time, but a fast-shrinking majority, yearly whittled down as world conditions change, and as people as a whole become more sensitive to suffering in all its forms – the changing attitude that White Eagle foresaw.*

Man is not equipped for tearing and devouring flesh. Nor has he the right kind of digestion for assimilating it; flesh putrefies in the bowels, whereas a more natural diet ferments. But to shun flesh eating is not enough without grasping what is implied by vegetarianism. No attempt can be made to discuss this fully here;† but it may be said that vegetarian foods can be far more sustaining, nourishing and attractive than flesh foods.

In reality the term vegetarian is a misnomer, because vegetables form only a part of the diet which also consists of fruits, nuts, wholemeal bread and other wholefoods. The term humanitarian more accurately describes the outlook and principles of the vegetarian. Not that the humanitarian mode of living is any too easy nowadays, when few foods escape denaturalisation by one or other of the so-called processing methods beloved by the manufacturer and chemist, who in hundreds of ingenious ways improve the appearance and increase the convenience of basic foodstuffs, but rob them of their vitality. Rats fed exclusively on white bread soon die. A dog fed largely on white bread, or on biscuits made from white flour, soon develops hysteria; but fed on baked wholemeal bread a dog will keep healthy and fit. Nor does the general use of artificial fertilisers in place of natural compost or manure make for health.

Foods that make for health are *whole* foods, such as bread made from the whole grain, legumes and vegetables, dairy produce, salads in great variety, honey, dark brown sugar, nuts of many kinds and flavours – all these in combination can fortify health.

* A strong case can be made against meat eating today, both on economic grounds and on the basis of the world food shortage. It is estimated that one acre of land will provide eleven times more protein as a direct crop than it will provide if the same land is used to graze cattle.
† The White Eagle Publishing Trust books SIMPLY DELICIOUS, NOT JUST A LOAD OF OLD LENTILS, THRIFTY FIFTY and BEANFEAST, all by Rose Elliot, are recommended not only for their hundreds of nutritious and delicious recipes, but for their store of information on the vegetarian way of life and food values, as well as on the many admirable alternatives to animal flesh that are now available.

What above all is at the root of so many of the present day ills of mankind? Man's largely unconscious cruelty – there we have it. For in this age organised cruelty has become part and parcel of existence, has become an accepted pattern of everyday life, so that no one even recognises it as cruelty, not even those who suffer under it.

Apart from the all too obvious cruelty and violence inflicted on men by their fellows, proclaimed each day through the media, there is the dreadful record of cruelty and exploitation of the animal world (which rebounds on to man in the end). And who can deny man's cruelty to mother earth herself, when he drains away her fertility by his get-rich-quick methods of agriculture, poisons her rivers with his factory wastes and leaves desolate acres behind him?

We have still to admit and accept how unwittingly cruel our thoughts can be, how readily we think or speak destructively about our fellows, without in the least realising what we are doing. Everyman is the culprit, and he is largely ignorant and therefore innocent of the realisation of any cruelty. His guilt only begins when he becomes aware of what is happening.

In this chapter is an element of sadness. There is also occasion for great hope. Side by side, and keeping step with man's manifold cruelties (so illogical is he) rise new and shining humanities, brought about since the two great wars. Thus does God ever bring forth good out of evil. Man no longer glorifies war, but hates and fears it. As never before he realises his own and his brothers' right to freedom from want, from care, from ignominy, from ignorance. Men and women are beginning to realise their responsibility to care for their fellow creatures. Ideals awaking in the human heart are already being translated into action. Each new year dawns with a promise which is sometimes equalled by its performance; man sees justification for hope and finds that many of his fears lack substance. Yet still it appears that the Satan of man's heedlessness and cruelty, and the God of his heartfelt dreams stand seemingly defying each other. But surely in God's sight good and evil do not really oppose each other, since evil and its resultant suffering must bring forth good, and good itself becomes better, stronger for having overcome evil? To regard the world thus, realising its evils but being duly thankful for its blessings, is a first step towards realisation of health; for it is a healthy outlook and brings that serenity of spirit which creates health. The healer will encounter patients whose bodily condition is a direct result of their way of life. He will be asked to help people who have committed many a dietetic sin (possibly in ignorance) while comfortably believing that their illnesses have been inflicted on them by God, though their bodily conditions are symptomatic of their disbelief in Him.

What is meant by a dietetic sin? Well, recently a patient came along who had lived mainly on a diet of meat washed down and pickled in her interior with milkless black tea, laced with lashings of white sugar and drunk scalding hot. That is a dietetic sin. Her complaints were manifold. You may well have patients, like this sufferer, healer-to-be. What are you going to do about her – about the type of sufferer who has eaten wrongly, exercised wrongly (or, more likely, never taken any), who has always thought wrongly and indulged in wrong feelings, and whose body is therefore in a chronically toxic state? Some patients will be like this – not all, but some; others will be normal and happy people easily cured.

What is to be done about the problem patients? You will find counsel later in the book. You cannot argue your patient into believing, or following, any advice you may give. Your part will be to wait and work on him. As time passes, in the measure you are helping him, and in the measure that he gets to know the real you during healing, so will he listen to a hint here, a suggestion there – reluctantly given, seemingly, so that he thinks he is finding matters out for himself. That is the way; but everything depends on what the healer has within himself.

Within himself? . . . This means purity of living. We come back again to White Eagle's words. How true it is that purity is supremely important in healing. What, then, of habits such as smoking and drinking?

Let it be remembered that a non-smoker or one who never drinks alcohol becomes very sensitive to another person's breath or clothes smelling of either. It is torture to some people to sit in, say, a railway refreshment car where people are drinking alcohol, eating flesh, or smoking. It would be unpleasant therefore for a sensitive patient like this to be treated by a healer who was himself smelling of smoke or drink. For his own sake and for the sake of his patient, he might forego both.

But White Eagle counsels moderation always. One should not be too rigid, too puritanical.

Digesting truth gradually
'People come to us seeking guidance on spiritual unfoldment, and we cannot always explain the principle governing these things. It is not always wise to hurl truth at your brother. So we try to give our brother or sister the amount of information that he or she can digest at that particular time; then we watch. If the pupil proves earnest, and tries to follow our simple rules, by degrees more and more is unfolded. There are various ways of helping people, and what helps one may not apply to another. There are, however, certain basic rules affecting man's physical well-being and spiritual training.

'First, food, to which some people pay far too much attention. Your food supplies nourishment not only to the physical but also to the etheric bodies; so if you eat and enjoy the foods nourished by the sun, such as sun-kissed fruits, sun-ripened whole corn, berries and nuts from the trees, you are feeding the higher, the aspiring atoms in your being, and thus assisting your spiritual unfoldment; whereas the grosser, coarser foods will make spiritual unfoldment more difficult. Nevertheless, it is not so much the food you eat but the nature of your thoughts and general outlook on life that matters. Remember that your bodies are the temple of the spirit, of the God within; and you should so live as to be attuned always to God, to good. In spiritual unfoldment always seek for harmony; always keep your elbows well in, physically, mentally, spiritually. But that is the soft, easy way, you say. Oh no, try it and see! It will require a long mental training to attune yourself harmoniously to life. . . .'

If a man gives all his goods to feed the poor, and lacks charity, we are told, he is nothing. He may also possess all knowledge concerning the origins of disease, be they spiritual or physical, and have abandoned all his bad habits – but lacking charity or love still be nothing as a healer. The measure of love that he bears towards his patient counts above all. For love beareth all things, hopeth all things, and endureth all things; and all comes back to this one issue, which lies between God and man. Without the Creator the creature can do nothing. Standing firm beside his Creator man takes on himself the measure of a man, and that man is Christ; and it is that Christ spirit in man which heals, comforts and redeems.

15

A TALK ABOUT MANY THINGS

Remember that your life should vibrate like a tuning fork. Strive to ring out with a clear pure note. In daily life, remain still and calm in your soul, so that your soul may sing in harmony with the music of the spheres. Live thus, and you will be conserving and not destroying the finer ethers which are your real home; so also will you be living to help and bless other lives.

W.E.

White Eagle continues to underline and amplify the theme of healthy living.

'If we told you to drink only natural rain or spring water, you would say this was impossible – as of course it is! So the next best thing is distilled water, which is freed from a residue of ash and earthy substance which, deposited in the body, in time induce rheumatism and similar ills.

'It is better for the healer to abstain from smoking; and if you can overcome the habit, the effort entailed contributes towards self-mastery, moreover without tobacco you will live longer and more healthily. This also applies in lesser degree to tea and coffee. I am only telling you what you will yourself learn one day. I do not suggest that you go home and vow that you will never again drink tea or coffee; but bear in mind that these things are eventually harmful, although your physical body has grown accustomed to them and your palate craves for them. The choice is yours, but remember that you are hoping to become channels for healing. Is your will to heal sufficiently strong to discipline your body and control your bodily appetites so that you become a pure and perfect channel for the healing power? Your reward will be your joy when you become true healers. . . .'

Diet for healers

'We know that many of you healers have to earn your daily bread in a workaday world of particular difficulty. If you were secluded in some monastery or temple, it would be easier for you. Many find it difficult to obtain other than flesh foods, while others believe meat eating to be essential to well-being. We do not agree that this is so; we think that meat eating is no more than a bad habit, and when the body accustoms itself to going without meat it gains much in health. We bear in mind however that despite the many efficient substitutes for meat, many a vegetarian lives unwisely; and also that many valuable vegetable foods are never eaten, or the most important portions of the vegetable are often thrown away. In this connection it is worth bearing in mind that as a general rule the plant which grows above ground is more valuable as a food than that which grows below, out of the sunlight. Leaves are therefore more valuable than roots.

'Nuts, dried and fresh fruits, honey (can you conceive a more beautiful food than honey, the very food of the gods!) rye and wholewheat biscuits and bread, the pulses in moderation – all these are foods with light and life in them. Milk is a fine food, but don't eat too much cheese, as many people do. Try pure grape juice for a week or two and note the results.

'Fresh and dried fruits are good, if eaten ripe and sweet; always choose wholemeal bread, but abstain from too much starch, which can clog the body and become a passive but a dangerous enemy. Refined sugar, too, is a mortal enemy. You do not realise, you who have long eaten too much, how little food is actually needed. The dietetic habits of your nation are peculiar, to say the least! Try gradually to shed the idea that concoctions of badly cooked and unappetising flesh and vegetables are essential to health, especially when so much of the value even of these foods is lost in water and steam.

'Eat only foods possessing the best food value, and you will feel better and more energised in every way. Vegetables of all kinds are good, and salads.

'As to fish? Well, those who wish to change over slowly to a vegetarian diet will find fish a good substitute for meat, a transition food. However if you can avoid flesh altogether you will develop far greater staying power, and far greater resistance to disease. . . .'

The holy breath

'All men, consciously or unconsciously, are seeking for the holy breath. We wonder how many realise its power, which is that of life, of wisdom and of love. There is so much to learn about the art of breathing, which can control your unfoldment and your health on the physical, mental and spiritual planes. Many people age prematurely because their bodies become charged with poisons accumulated during the whole life – poison resulting from eating the wrong food, from inhaling impure air and from failure properly to exhale such air. Watch yourself. Do you breathe only with the top of the lungs, leaving an accumulation of stale air in the lower lungs? This habit may continue for a whole life time, and now is the time to correct it. If you will follow exactly the simple practice we are going to suggest you will find only good will result, but don't strain in any way. All breathing exercise should be harmonious and without discomfort; it should bring a sense of well-being.

'Each morning, on rising, stand, if possible, before an open window. Relax your body and breathe slowly, quietly, harmoniously, first exhaling till the lungs are completely empty, then gradually drawing the breath deeper until you are filling the lower part of the lungs and expanding the ribs as you breathe. Then exhale again, drawing in the abdomen, until once more the lungs are completely empty. As you inhale each breath, aspire to God – feel that God is entering into you; as you exhale, bless all life. By this inbreathing you are drawing spiritual light into your heart centre. It is like bringing spiritual sunlight and refreshment to the seed atom resting in your heart. You are filling every particle of your being with God's breath. As you do this you will naturally be freed from earthly problems because you will forget your body and for a fleeting moment be released. Always when you breathe thus, you will find relief from the bondage of cares and limitations.

'Repeat this simple exercise several times, for as long as you like, as often as you like, but always without strain.

'By now you will probably be thinking: But what about all the impurities in the atmosphere? You will not breathe in any harm if you concentrate on the breath of God, of good. . . .'

The gifts of God

'We emphasise again the value of pure thought, pure food, pure water, fresh air, sunlight, warmth, all the elements which constitute the growing power, the creative power in nature. Flowers, herbs, fruits, vegetables, all these are the product of the divine Intelligence and Power working in Mother Earth to produce the perfect food for man. The simpler your life, the better healer you will become. We mean by this not only simplicity and purity of the food you eat, but the air you breathe, the water you drink and with which you cleanse your body, and the sunshine which warms you and stimulates the life forces in you. All these gifts are as your brothers, part of you, part of God.

'May every day of life find you, our beloved healer, when you rise in the morning, opening the windows of your soul to the sunlight. Even in winter the whole atmosphere is impregnated with tiny atoms of invisible sunlight, and when you breathe deeply, consciously breathing in the sunlight of God, you grow in well-being, in loving kindliness to all life; and also you will begin to become aware of the power of the invisible forces which you may contact. The healer must learn how to open himself to the sunlight and how to purify his bodies so that he may contact the angelic influence.

'When the soul lives in the consciousness of the Infinite Spirit, that soul must becomes harmonious in all ways. He does not overstrain any part of the physical body, for he is harmoniously attuned to the rhythm of life. He does not break the laws of nature; he lives harmoniously with natural law. He breathes deeply of the fresh air, and frequently. He uses water lavishly, for water does not only cleanse the physical body, it also purifies the etheric body. It is a good thing to have water in your healing sanctuary, and for healers to sip a little water. Correct and deep breathing is so important too to the healer, who must remember and believe that he is breathing the creative power, the purifying element into the physical body. All the laws of nature are observed by the healer who is attuned to his Source. He should not take too much food, but certainly sufficient to sustain and give the energy that is necessary. His mind should be in harmony with Divine Spirit, not agitated, overpressed, or indecisive, but quiet and still so that it can become a perfect instrument for that creative and all-healing power.

'We know, my dear brethren, that this is a gospel of perfection but it is good to remember and try to practise the precepts of this gospel. When man can do this, the lessons which he has to learn in the physical body are learnt without the necessity of illness or inharmony. We know perfectly all the excuses of the mind of earth: "How can I do this, how can I do the other when I'm so driven, here, there and everywhere?" That may be so, but deep, deep within you is the centre of stillness and calmness, and if you can remember to withdraw to that centre of stillness your body will not become overstrained or tired – whatever your tasks, there will be no ill results in your physical state.

'When healing, don't think about pouring out your own personal healing power, but rather think of receiving the cosmic rays which you are confident will stream through your hands. The hands of the healer are centres for the passage of such rays of healing.'

The etheric body
We now come back to the subject of the etheric body, already briefly touched upon in an earlier chapter.

White Eagle says: 'The etheric body is a counterpart of the physical interpenetrating it. The etheric body is intimately related to the nervous system, and indeed has its own counterpart of the physical nervous system. We find in the etheric body certain centres of force; these are primarily centres for the etheric body, but have their counterpart in the physical, and are gateways for the divine life force to flow into the physical body.

'The main centres lie, first, at the brow between and a little above the eyes. Then, the crown and the base of the brain; the throat centre can be approached either from the back of the neck or from the front, where the little hollow lies. The heart centre is in the middle of the breast, and not slightly to the left as is the physical heart. Then there is the solar plexus centre – so often connected with digestive troubles, and more sensitive to thought than any other centre; and the spleen, just below the ribs on the left of the body. Finally there is the centre at the base of the spine. There are also other lesser centres through which the healing light can be poured, but we are not concerned with these at the moment. All these centres are largely dormant in the spiritually unawakened man, but as man begins to develop and unfold spiritually, so these centres of force in the etheric body become vibrant and beautiful.

'We have said that the basis of all sickness lies in the etheric body, which is the bridge or transmitting link from the spiritual to the material. That is to say, the life force enters the physical body through the centres of the etheric body. Where there is inharmony or disturbance in the etheric body, there follows a block in the transmission of this life force; in consequence, the physical body weakens and even dies. The task of the healer is to learn how to re-establish this flow of life force. As he offers himself as a transmitting agent, it follows that he must strive to become a pure channel. His mind should be tranquil and harbour no criticism or condemnation. He should set apart a period daily for meditation, and learn to govern haste, fear and anger.

'Seek for that which you have in common with your patient, which is the Divine Spirit, and so let your own spirit meet and mingle with his. Get that essential point of contact if you can; get past the outer shell; reach towards his innermost self – the life within. In time you will learn to do this naturally, effortlessly. Then the life force, the vital force, can be poured through you to him. The patient often cannot by himself open himself to the light, but once you have made that contact with his spirit, you who are his healer may be able to transmit the force without hindrance.

'We prefer the least possible handling of the patient, with not too many passes. All depends, of course, on the circumstances of the case; but, generally speaking, the trained and experienced healer will utilise the spiritual ray and concentrate on the vital centres. Let your touch be very light. Remember, you are working mainly on the etheric, the aura of which stands out from the physical. The whole idea of healing is to restore peace and harmony, and then to recharge the patient with spiritual light and power. When making passes to clear the aura always work downwards, and off at the feet. You may pour in the life force from your two hands placed on the soles of his feet – much help may be given this way; you may also pour in power through the patient's hands.

'True healing takes place on the spiritual plane, and healing power comes from the Christ sphere. According to the purity of the healer, it pours through his subtler vehicles and streams from his hands and indeed from his whole aura. Healing depends not so much on the laying-on of hands, but on a clear and full contact with Christ; the essence of Christ can then pour forth from the whole aura and can be intensified in its actions by the healer's mental control. This is the true healing.'

16

'HERE I STAND, EMPTY, LORD; FILL THOU ME!'

*When we speak of light we mean God. God is love; light is
love. Love is light. Understand that through attuning your
mind and emotions every day you can utilise the substance of
light. Indeed, you are already making use of it; for to a degree
you are absorbing it, and moulding it into your bodies.*

W.E.

It will be seen by now that neither magnetic healing by passes to
clear the aura, nor yet manipulation of the etheric body of the
patient by the etheric hands of the healer in order to loosen up
deep-seated complaints, constitute in themselves a complete
healing. They prepare the way; they can alleviate or remove pain,
inflammation and general physical disarray; but the true, real and
lasting healing presupposes the addition of something vital and
essential which is the crux of the whole. What can this be?

On almost every page of White Eagle's message the answer has
been given. It is as applicable to the healer as to the patient. Both
must prepare themselves to receive it. Both must be faithful to it
by the practice of the presence of God, not by infrequent and
sporadic effort, but constantly, continually, consciously, until the
intake of the spiritual light becomes habitual, as natural and as
necessary as breathing or the circulation of the blood. It is in this
blood stream, which is etheric as well as physical, which is
literally life in circulation, that the Presence operates, renewing it
and thereby renewing the man. In spiritual healing this is one of
the methods of recharging the sick with new and more abundant
life.

We cannot too clearly define the missing factor that is required
to perfect our healing. It is that for which the healer is bidden to
purify himself in order that he may receive. It is Christlike; it is

indeed the light and power of Christ, of God, which can fill the soul of the healer and can radiate from him, pour through him into the soul – that is, to the invisible bodies – of his patient. The healer has to open himself by prayer, devotion, and surrender of himself in order that he may receive the divine light. That light may appear to him as a glorious sun shining down on him, shining down into him, filling him with its golden radiance; or it may appear to him as the figure of the Master, come close with outstretched hands and shining face. From those two hands rays of healing stream to the healer.

With a sense of power and presence such as this does he lay his hand on his patient. With such a sense of incoming light and power does he transmit this radiance, or pour it into his patient, dispelling and replacing darkness by light. Nor is this all. There may be other seats of darkness needing illumination; in the patient's body mind, for instance, or in the head mind. Who knows what accumulation of enshadowed thoughts and gloom have congregated in those two minds? Both can be treated with the spiritual light and power which, like golden sunshine, can be poured into, say, the solar plexus (which is the headquarters of the emotions), or at the forehead.

True, miracles are not wrought in a moment. Illnesses which have brooded in the body or head long before they seized on some region of the physical body are not dispelled for ever by one treatment; nor are the accumulated fears habitual to those two minds. Patience, devotion, sacrifice – these are the watchwords which open the gate of healing. Nevertheless, a start can be made, even in the first treatment. The patient can be cleansed, the grip of his complaint loosened, and he can receive the light. One thing remains, and this is possibly the most important of all. For most of us when we fall sick in body feel also sick at heart. We know too well that something has gone wrong, not only in the mortal body but within ourselves. We want the healing touch deeply within ourselves – those infinitely tender and sensitive selves which we believe we successfully conceal from everyone, even from our own consciousness. What we long for, even unconsciously, is to be aware of the love of God.

This is where the healer can give true help; for he can transmit, to however limited a degree, something of that love; he can treat the heart centre – if necessary without touching his patient – the spiritual heart situated at the centre of the breast. Instead of pouring in rays of golden spiritual light, as he has done previously, he can now open himself to receive a rose-coloured light (spiritual light, like physical light, possesses all the colours of the spectrum) and transmit this rose light to the heart centre of his patient. Rose is the colour of divine love. Divine love can comfort and heal the sick at heart.

And now a word of caution. Supposing the healer is trying to wean somebody away from drink or drugs; would it be legitimate for him to pray for the enslaved victim, to argue with him if necessary, and try to set his thinking right – in fact to use all normal and reasonable means to detach him from his addiction? Yes; but it would be utterly wrong for any healer to try to win that victim back to sobriety by dominating him, by imposing his own will power and subduing that of the victim, thereby making him subservient to his healer. This is what Christian Scientists call 'mental malpractice'. Any such methods could be harmful both to healer and sufferer, and would impose a heavy karmic debt on the former.

All the foregoing is equally applicable to sickness. The healer must never be dominated by his patient's sickness – indeed he must feel that he is master of it. But he may never interfere with the freewill choice of his patient. Should that patient have taken refuge in sickness and, subconsciously, does not really want to get well – and there are many in this state – he may be reasoned with, prayed for, and may be treated by having spiritual light and love poured into one or other of his centres, perhaps at the solar plexus, the heart or the head. But he may not be *willed* by the healer to do anything. His mind must not be mentally imposed on, he must not be mentally bullied. Such things can happen. Any form of hypnotic influence is as foreign to spiritual healing as is mental domination of the patient.

This brings up yet another question which was shelved during the first part of the book. An imaginary questioner wanted to know whether any explanation could be found for the premature and painful death of a dearly loved friend whose life to him had seemed blameless. What justice or reason could be seen in such a death? In short, what was God thinking about to let such things happen within His universe?

This, of course, brings up the age-old problem of the so-called innocent suffering, and is in effect a challenge to belief in a beneficent God. It casts doubt on the loving kindness of God towards every one of His children. Would it be proper to suggest that the death might have had other causes than the heedlessness of God? The inharmonies and stressful conditions which make for ill health and the shortening of many lives are created by man, and not by God. Is it therefore right or fair to shelve the trouble we bring on ourselves by blaming the good Lord? Surely, if we expect justice from God we should at least be reasonable and fair in our treatment of God?

However, these are only minor contributory reasons for ill health. Why then did this good person die so painfully, when it has been said by White Eagle that within the bounds of karmic law all illness is curable? Let us admit that the enforced discipline of illness can bring blessing to the soul, perhaps subduing pride, or humbling vanity. A prolonged illness can indeed sweeten an obdurate character, softening the heart and teaching lasting humility. This happens when some karmic debt is faced fairly and squarely; when its discharge is accompanied by a change of heart, the debt having provided the soul with an opportunity by which it has richly profited. Against this, there are some whom illness embitters. They harden themselves against God and their fellow creatures. Nevertheless, no man escapes the law. The hardening heart only incurs additional suffering because it draws additional suffering towards itself by its reaction to life. So much it can bear, and after that no more. The heart breaks at last – to use the old-fashioned term; and into that breaking heart God enters, for this is God's long awaited opportunity. No soul can forever evade God.

None of this, however, applies here, our questioner will say, although he will admit that in some few cases illness can serve so valuable a purpose that to heal it might even be against the sufferer's true interest. Then illness comes to the sufferer as friend rather than foe. It has been said that even when everything else fails to soften a heart, continued illness will do so. Our questioner's answer to this is that his loved one was always gentle and loving. To this problem there is yet an answer, and in that answer a justification of God.

A few souls at certain stages of their life journey arrive at some crucial changing or turning point. They have previously lived average sort of lives; they have proceeded from one average life to another. Occasionally, however, something more than a good average citizen is required. An age just dawning may need a saint, a martyr, a leader, a teacher. Such qualities of soul and character are evolved through deep and sometimes painful experience. Prolonged illness and painful death faced with indomitable courage, unflagging cheerfulness and patience, is, rightly seen, an initiation, through which the soul acquires powers and qualities hitherto unknown, and by which the soul is nobly equipped for its future, gaining power to help and bless mankind.

How far such an answer as this will satisfy our questioner is a matter he alone can decide. Yet most of us when we look back can recall some so-called tragedy affecting the life and even the death of folk whom we have loved and revered; and in the light of time can see how that suffering was the means of bringing good either to the sufferer or to those around him. Perhaps it is only our shortsightedness which prevents us seeing how wonderfully the wisdom and love of God is outworking through pain and tribulation.

17

FORGIVE AND BE FORGIVEN

If you will train yourself to think in terms of love and forgiveness every moment of your life, a most beautiful healing will take place in you.

W.E.

Part II has served in some degree to indicate the path to be followed by the true spiritual healer; although that is not to say that he must adopt so rigorous a training immediately, or think that without it he cannot heal. No, he can be a channel for the healing power from the beginning. But as he learns more about himself, so will he learn about the factors in himself that hinder his healing.

We now come to the question of absent healing. Contact healing by its very nature is limited by time and space; but to absent healing there is no such limitation and this is perhaps why this aspect of the healing as practised in the White Eagle Lodge has grown vastly over the years.* It will be apparent from the brief description in Chapter 2 that this should not be thought of as faith healing, or as healing by prayer in the accepted sense of the word – say, by the voicing of petitions to the Almighty to make sick people well. The work is undertaken by groups, trained in the use of thought power, taught how to project, from their own soul, the Christ power of light and healing. They are working in conscious co-operation with unseen helpers. Who are these helpers? Those working in the healing groups have come to know them as angels – angels of healing. The form of service in use by the groups (its wording was given by White Eagle) invokes these angelic powers, and at the same time helps the sitters in the group

* See Postscript.

to become attuned to the healing angels and receptive to their power which is then projected to the sick and those in need. The group directs the healing to the patient by the vibration of the spoken word – that is, by the leader repeating the name of the sick person slowly and deliberately, several times. Each name is sounded as a call to the patient, making a link with his soul on the inner etheric plane. It matters not at all where that person lives, a distance of a mile or a thousand miles makes no difference. The groups are working in the soul world which is a world of thought, and in the same way as the spoken word can encircle the globe in the fraction of a second by radio, so the vibration of a name spoken in the healing chapel reaches out across space (etheric space) and the soul of the person called becomes attentive and alert to what is happening, ready to receive the healing ray. (He has already been told how to tune in and become receptive.) This ray affects his soul rather than his mind, bringing an inner feeling of well-being which presently translates itself into improved health of the body. It is better that there should be conscious co-operation on the part of the patient, but if he is too ill to tune in, some relative can do so on his behalf. When the soul has been alerted and the link made, the healing ray is directed to sensitive points in the etheric body of the patient – the etheric centres described in Chapter 15.

With constant repetition the words of the absent healing service accumulate a special quality. They become like a mantram. In time, too, the sitters in these absent healing groups become deeply attuned, and their projection gets very powerful; they often become sensitively aware of the response of their patients, for when working with the invisible, one's sensitivity quickly increases. In much the same way does the sick person increasingly respond to the healing ray sent out by the group.

There is no question of blind faith here, for long experience of the working of these groups has demonstrated how real and exact a practice it is. There is no need, be it physical, mental or spiritual, that the power of absent healing is unable to reach. People can be helped through ordeals or strengthened spiritually to cope with problems of everyday life. Sick animals respond, often miraculously; even haunted houses can be cleared of obsessing entities. The healers give their services weekly, year in and year out, fulfilling their weekly obligations with great regularity, assured beyond all doubt that their work is blessed. A spiritual urge seems to pervade the group, so that the sitters feel spiritually renewed and sustained afterwards, and come again and yet again willingly, even eagerly. As a result they themselves develop spiritually and so live more healthfully and happily – an unfoldment or development which is a natural outcome of spiritual service.

The results of this method of healing speak for themselves and are a constant source of encouragement to the healers. The following have been selected by the Healing Secretary from files containing records of thousands of cases because they demonstrate the scope of absent healing.

A child, G.A. Healing was asked for this child. The child suffered from leukaemia, a disease from which there is considered to be no recovery. From the outset of the treatment he began to improve, and after nine months – to the surprise of the doctors – his blood count was normal and he was attending school as usual. Six months later a specialist reported that they now regarded the child as normal, and that his recovery had been a miracle.

In this case neither the child nor the parents knew that the absent treatment was being given. The request came through the friend of a friend of the family, who tuned in on the child's behalf.

A woman, E.H. Healing was requested for this patient by her sister. She suffered from a disease of the liver and kidneys, and an internal haemorrhage which was later diagnosed as cirrhosis of the liver. She was expected to pass on at any time. For a while, the doctors could not understand what was keeping her alive, but after some two years not only was she still alive, but the disease, according to the X ray, appeared to have been arrested. Later the report came in that the doctors considered hers to be a miracle case. The patient states quite simply that she knows where her strength comes from.

A girl, S.H. The patient was diagnosed as suffering from

schizophrenia and had entered a mental hospital. From the first treatment the change in the patient was marked. She was soon home again, and is now leading an active and happy life, taking part in club activities and generally behaving in a normal, well-adjusted manner. Her family were amazed at her immediate response to spiritual healing.

The minister of a London church was being literally persecuted by a poltergeist in a church hall which he used for various meetings, particularly those of a youth club. The creature was mischievous, throwing articles about, breaking them and generally causing eerie disturbances. Here is a different type of case, which also responded very well; the groups have treated several similar cases, always with complete success. As soon as the building was placed on an absent healing group, and special treatment given, the trouble lessened, and in the course of a few months cleared up completely.

A man, P.R., wrote from a Welsh hospital asking for absent healing, because he had been so impressed with its effect on a boy brought into a neighbouring bed after a serious motor bicycle crash. P.R. himself had been involved in a car accident some time previously, and the many broken bones in his case were obstinately refusing to heal. In three months he reported that since being on the group he had made good progress, and that, after all, no bone grafting had been necessary. He subsequently recovered completely, a slight stiffness in the right leg being the only ill effects of an accident which caused him to break a leg, an arm, and his jaw in two places.

These few cases demonstrate the scope of absent healing and suggest that nothing is impossible to the powers of the spirit. Nobody can tell how a case is going to respond. Miracles happen, sometimes to those ignorant that they are receiving healing. Whatever the results, the healers continue faithfully with their work year in and year out, in quiet faith and assurance that they are co-operating with the Christ spirit in healing human suffering.

One major factor in healing has as yet hardly been stressed. That factor is the human body's capacity to forgive its owner even when that person has long sinned against it; for a lot of us take more care of our home or garden, our business or career, our hobbies and pursuits, our motor car, or anything else extraneous to our bodies, than we do of poor brother body. Have you ever seen a neglected dog chained up outside some lonely house or farm, say, as a watch dog? Once daily, perhaps, somebody feeds this dog with scraps. It matters little whether those scraps are wholesome food for dogs. The dog gulps them down, since it is given nothing better to eat. Once a day, perhaps, the dog is let off the chain for a run. Then it gets into mischief, naturally enough, and is cursed as a ne'er-do-well.

Or have you ever seen an ageing and neglected horse grazing in a paddock with little enough to eat? It is obviously over-worked. Its coat stares and is matted with old dirt and sweat. Its knees are sadly broken by ancient cuts, caused by falls when overdriven. Beneath its collar are recent sores, and its skin is galled in several places. There is little covering on its ribs and its head droops. Yet with its owner behind it, and flogged by a sharp word and sharper whip, that horse will go until it drops, so game is its spirit.

What purpose do such descriptions serve? Only this: have we not known people who ill-treat their bodies, perhaps not to the same extent, but who are neglectful, unsympathetic, and even cruel to them; and who in consequence have been crippled with sickness or even died prematurely?

Let us suppose that we were in a position to adopt this ill-used dog or horse; let us suppose we took the creature home and fed and loved and exercised it sufficiently and wisely enough to keep our pet obedient and disciplined. Can anyone doubt that the animal's response would be a hundredfold in devotion and fidelity? Or that we, its new master or mistress, would take legitimate pride and joy in its high spirits, energy, health and affection? Whither is all this leading us? Surely, to the realisation that those of us who have forgotten the rights of poor brother body (and brother body mind) have still an opportunity to win back affection and forgiveness.

Sooner or later all those who disregard the body are forced to try to remedy its ills. Whenever this is done reluctantly and with a grievance, any good attempted is undone because the body will not co-operate. Whenever it is done lovingly – well, there is a difference.

It will be the manner of our future thinking and feeling about our body which will determine whether or not it will co-operate with us. Several of our Lord's parables cover this very point, including a special petition in the Lord's Prayer regarding forgiveness. We cannot get away from this necessity for forgiveness, nor yet regain health until we ourselves forgive.

This present book must not set forth any theory and practice of healing without some record of the results obtained. Its third part will therefore consist of this record, written by a healer who has long practised healing as set forth by White Eagle, and will give results, not as a list of unqualified successes, but more as an enquiry into the reasons underlying either success or failure. It has never been suggested that this method of healing can by itself cure every complaint. The ruling factor is ever the patient's power of response. However, the proportion of cures is so impressive that it cannot be ignored, particularly since many of these involve patients who have been declared incurably ill by medicine; for spiritual healing is often the last resort of the desperately ill.

Finally, in a world where sickness abounds, our hope and prayer is that readers will find, as they read these pages, a quiet assurance of God's goodness, and learn that it is the hand of God which heals, and the heart of God which blesses, and without God there is no well-being for man.

Part III

Some Healing Cases

18

A CURE OF CANCER

*Take with both hands that which the world calls bitterness,
for within the bitterness is the nectar, the sweetness. From every
experience you will gather delicate and beautiful flowers. It is
the way you accept your experiences that matters; the way
you use them, the way you allow them to awaken within
your heart the love of the Christ spirit.*

W.E.

Whether this third part can be written to my own satisfaction –
let alone that of my readers – remains to be seen. One reason for
this misgiving is that I have never kept any record of my healing
practice otherwise than in a fairly retentive memory.

Let me start by repeating earnestly that by myself, by my own
power alone, I have never healed anyone. Unaided I can do
nothing; I depend on invisible help, which I have always consciously and earnestly sought, and it has always come. Through
me that power has healed men and women – how many I forget –
but for half a working life.

The reader will ask about the nature of this power: what it is,
where it comes from, who or what provides it. The question will
best be answered by citing a number of cases as examples of what
can be done, starting with my worst case, one of cancer. Here I
would say that sometimes the terrifying name and reputation of a
disease in itself arrests a cure. No healer must ever be scared by a
name or by a condition.

The patient in this case was a boy of about twelve who had
cancer of the jaw. Part of the jaw had been removed by a surgeon,
leaving the face sadly disfigured. However, the disease had only
been temporarily checked and was now making rapid progress,
so that the boy was only expected to live for a few weeks. The
stricken parents had not wholly abandoned hope that spiritual

healing might help their son, and it was arranged that the boy's father and I should give him healing on alternate days.

It was a most distressing case. The boy's condition was so desperate, the disease so grievous that its odour seemed to impregnate the whole house. Lying in bed, the boy could not be disturbed, so that all a healer could do was to clear the boy's aura as he lay, and to keep on clearing the aura, over and over again, putting all his spiritual power and concentration into the passes, and praying that something of the light and the power would remain. Afterwards, although I wore a white linen coat which was washed after each treatment, and although I washed my face, hands and arms, I used to return home feeling really ill because the condition had so permeated my own aura. A bath and a complete change of clothes could only partly remove the feeling.

As I said, the boy's father and I worked by turns. For some weeks there was no apparent change in the patient's condition, except that he held his own. Then he started to sweat, usually at night; the sweating became so violent as to necessitate a change not only of his night attire, but also of the bedclothes, several times during the night. This sweating continued for some time, during which he lost more weight. But now his appetite began to assert itself and presently he began to eat heartily, and later enormously. At the same time the sweating declined, and he regained strength rapidly, while his face took on colour and a natural appearance, and the characteristic odour of the disease departed. Treatments were continued until the recovery seemed complete, and the boy was his healthy, natural self again.

More recently I have been in touch with another cancer case. This time it was a middle-aged woman suffering from a growth in the breast. For some time she received healing treatments for this growth, and also took crude black molasses, which some people regard as a specific for cancer, at any rate in its early stages. (I cannot confirm this save only in this one instance.*)

Our patient was also under the care of a naturopath, largely because her general health had become undermined by realisation

---

* A booklet by Cyril Scott deals with this subject, and is called CRUDE BLACK MOLASSES. It is on sale at health food stores.

of the nature of the complaint. She tried to believe she had faith; but she had yet to be healed of her partial unbelief. Under her doctor's treatment her general condition improved, but the local condition appeared to be neither better nor worse; finally the doctor advised an operation, and his patient nerved herself for the ordeal. The result was happy; instead of some far-reaching growth being uncovered, the cancer was found to have so con- tracted that it was removed in its entirety by a comparatively minor operation, and the patient was pronounced clear of any likelihood of a recurrence of the disease.

So here is another happy issue. All the same, I can only repeat that advanced cases of cancer are unsuitable for treatment because of the excessive strain imposed on the healer. Such cases are better undertaken by absent healing groups, and this always in conjunction with medical treatment.

Cancer is one of those complaints which should never happen. Admitted, there are cases where death comes as a culmination, an initiation to a fuller, nobler existence, for such an illness met with sublime patience, courage and a selfless cheerfulness, frees the soul utterly from that particular karmic debt, gives it a deep new quality of consciousness so that in a new life it starts afresh on some brighter path. Thus the Divine Power brings forth good out of man's sore evil. Yet cancer remains as a disease which man aggravates and even invites by his ignorance of his own real nature and origin. Man must practise the presence of God to rid himself of cancer.

Man must grow closer to nature and by so doing closer to God. He cannot afford to do otherwise. God is a constant source of human vitality, a life stream which man may draw upon for every need, once he is attuned to receive from it. The constant practice of the presence of God, then, is a preventive and cure for all disease. No miracle drug, potion, injection, or anything else can supplant or replace the vitality emanating from God. Man is gradually living longer, because his body and mind have become less animal, less physical; they have become more sensitive, more responsive, more subtle; therefore he provides himself with a better-wearing body.

A frequent cause of bad health is ill-fitting clothing which hampers and restricts the body's freedom. Clamping clothes around the waist, so that their weight and pressure restricts circulation and digestion, can in the course of years cause trouble; this applies also to pressure on the body by arm bands, garters, girdles or belts of any kind. The effects are not felt during youth, but are stored up until middle or old age. Ill-fitting or high-heeled shoes promise not only the possibility of feet painful to live with, but also internal troubles caused by the body having been thrown out of balance over a number of years. Always, be it remembered, it is we ourselves who must dwell in our ill-used bodies, and suffer their pains and shortcomings.

Some time ago I was helping with a group of fourteen patients awaiting treatment. I had to find out their state of health, the nature of their complaints, and to select a healer for each patient. My task was complicated, for several patients suffered from not one but numerous bodily complaints; these had in turn been engendered or fostered by several etheric troubles or ailments, which had themselves arisen because of some deep spiritual inharmony.

One patient especially stands out in my mind. She was a woman in her seventies, perhaps, her face deeply lined with pain and patience – that is, she had retained an element of gentleness and kindliness which had enabled her to bear suffering patiently. Her trouble was varicose veins in one of her legs, veins in such a state that they must have given her constant and severe pain. Her leg was heavily bandaged. She had had two or three healing treatments and said her leg was better; yet I knew that this could not be more than temporary relief, for the trouble lay much deeper. Let me attempt to indicate how much deeper and you will perhaps grasp how tough a proposition this patient was.

Presumably the veins in that leg would never have enlarged had the blood stream been healthy and pure, when it would have maintained good healthy channels for itself. Why then did the blood stream deteriorate? Was it because of, say, constipation, that commonest of ailments of the flesh eater, which can creep on and poison its victim so insidiously? Quite likely, and also likely that the trouble was aggravated by her job, which involved much standing. Assuming constipation to be a partial cause, how did this arise? Very likely because of diet, if it is recalled how devitalised is the diet available to most of us. But diet cannot account for everything. God can overcome even a bad diet. There will have been a predisposing cause more powerful. I felt that cause to be a chronic and habitual fearfulness, corroding anxieties sunk deeply into the body mind of the victim; a lifelong fear of a harsh outer world. Yes, fear of God and man, fear of every circumstance in life, were written on that face.

Fear can arrest digestion, cause a hold-up, a blockage in the life stream, the life forces; in other words the basic cause of this woman's illness was spiritual lack, because of fear woven into the very fabric of the body itself; and that fear would never have victimised this poor woman had she possessed knowledge of God, since to know God is to trust God. Nevertheless, the problem was still there. The doctors had sought long and devotedly to help and heal this woman, and could do no more. Her case had been declared hopeless.

She was not alone, unfortunately. Of the fourteen sick persons dealt with that night several more had reached a similar position, in that they had been given up as incurable by orthodox medicine and had come seeking spiritual healing more or less as a last resort.

The second case was a woman in late middle age. Her immediate trouble was a growth in the nose, which again had probably arisen because of the clogging of the sinus and nasal passages by excessive catarrh. Catarrh, however, is the ultimate manifestation of what is in reality an etheric complaint due to a hold-up in the circulation of the psychic forces around the body a psychic circulation coincident with that of the blood stream. Here a knowledge of the psychic centres becomes important, for at one of these centres we shall find the hold-up which causes the catarrh.

A healer, in the course of time, gets a feeling for these things, so that when he lays his hands on a patient he becomes aware of what is wrong *etherically* with that patient, although this sensitivity takes some years to develop. So with this patient who had a sinus problem I became aware, when I touched her throat centre, where the trouble lay in her etheric body. I saw that there had long been a hold-up at this point, so much so that it had affected the physical body, which had become locked into a kind of rigidity, a board-like feeling at the back of the neck and shoulders.

What causes this locking at the throat centre, this etheric arrest which in due course becomes a very real, troublesome and sometimes serious complaint? Often, as with the first patient, it is fear – one of the hardest enemies to overcome.

With every sickness, you come back to this one answer. Something has arrested the vital flow, and the task of the spiritual healer is to restore it. The quiet beauty of the healing chapel will start the process. Here the patient can relax, can sink into rest, as it were, into the atmosphere of peace, of harmony and healing. Within the chapel are unseen healing powers and presences waiting to be called upon. The healing treatment is in itself relaxing, and to those who can give themselves wholly to it, can prove a wonderful experience. These factors combine to influence the mind and to exert some restorative effect on even the worst ailments. Little by little the moorings of the mind, which have been anchored down to sickness, become slackened. Maybe the patient begins to read the White Eagle books and finds in them a new faith, a new certainty of divine love so that his deepest fears begin to melt away. The slow process of spiritual rehabilitation begins to operate. Disease in the body is so often the final manifestation of causes lying very deep, and has been building up over a very long period. The spiritual healer is treating causes not symptoms, and the healing process can therefore be slow. Nevertheless, it is probable that most patients will in a few months' time become healthier, happier and more useful people. I have seen this happen too often not to be convinced that any patient can be cured, given time; often a considerable time – and on occasions a very long time indeed.

19

THE BOY WHO SLASHED DOWN FLOWERS

The wise do not grieve for those who have passed into the great beyond. The wise rejoice because they know that the beloved brother or sister, father, mother, husband, wife or child has gone into a world of freedom from pain, of light and beauty. The wise do not grieve for those living here, for life on earth has one purpose only – for the soul to learn through experience the power and love of God. Though some experience can be very painful, all things work together for good when the heart is set upon God.

W.E.

Sometimes one case of healing makes a lasting impression, remembered long after other, more recent cases, have been forgotten. This particular case happened a long time ago when I was young and inexperienced. The patient was a boy, brought to me by his mother. He was about ten years old, and eyed me in a sullen, dogged way indicative of toughness, yet there was an element of pathos in the child, a touch of bewilderment. His mother explained that she could do nothing with him, so changed had he become from the obedient and affectionate child he had been. Now he was a 'real bad boy', who took pleasure in tormenting his sisters, was spiteful to other children; and when out for a walk delighted in slashing down the wayside flowers with his stick, as an expression of his defiance and aggressiveness. Further enquiry brought out the fact that all this had begun shortly after the boy had had his tonsils removed in hospital. There had been something of a scene at the outset, the lad's cries and struggles having been so desperate that he had had to be held down until he finally succumbed to the anaesthetic. He came home a changed boy. His mother said that not even his father could do anything with him. The doctor had given the boy some medicine which had kept him a bit quieter, but hadn't done much good otherwise. Rightly speaking, he ought to have gone back to school, but his mother didn't like to send him now, not knowing what he might get up to.

The boy sat there, defiance in every inch of him, while I stood hesitating. I have no great power of clairvoyant vision, but even then had some faculty for locating a trouble by sense of touch, my hands having a sensitivity which seems to lead me to the spot; and when my hands touched that boy at the back of the neck – at the throat centre or chakra – I knew where the trouble lay.*

It was obvious to the etheric hand's touch that the boy's aura had become damaged at that point. The aura of a healthy person has a vibrancy, a resilience, while the unhealthy aura is flabby and thin. At the back of the boy's neck the aura just wasn't there – a state of affairs which gave a peculiar feeling of nakedness to the neck. The flesh of that boy's neck and shoulders had acquired an insensitivity, a deadness. Now I began to understand what had happened to him during his shouting and struggling before the operation on the throat. The shock and strain of it had torn or ruptured the aura, leaving him exposed to attack at this vital psychic throat centre. I wonder if I can explain what this sort of attack involves.

We humans are a very mixed crowd. Some of us are bad, some good; most of us are just middling. There are some crude, clumsy, thoughtless, ignorant and even brutal people about, some of whom play 'practical jokes' on their fellows which can also be crude and brutal. All of us are creating by our thoughts and feelings a thought world in which we live. Into that thought world discarnate entities, sometimes of a lower order, can have entry in certain circumstances. Human thought in itself can be powerful and lively enough on occasion to take temporary form and become what is called an elemental. As a bank holiday crowd scatters a common or woodland with its litter, so humanity casts

* The centres are all attached to the spine, and some – such as the throat, and sometimes the heart – can be more easily reached from the back, through the spine.

off a kind of 'thought litter'. The average person is shut away from this by the protective power of his own aura, but should that aura become damaged, as with this boy, the way is open for undesirable entities and thought forms to enter.

This lad's sensibilities had become exposed to attack from the thought world because of his damaged aura. Crude and un-developed creatures, with perhaps rather an unfortunate sense of humour or with mischievous intent, had fastened on to him. He had no spiritual source to which he could turn for protection, his parents knowing and caring little about religion.

The treatment was simple. The links with those undesirable elements in the thought world had to be cut, and then with the hands – both physical and etheric – drawn together to seal the torn edges of the aura. All this would be accomplished by an effort of the heart mind. The next task was to strengthen and replenish the body at its weakened throat centre by pouring in spiritual power like golden sunlight; and finally to seal that point of entry in order to forbid further entry to undesirable influences. This completed the first treatment. After about half a dozen weekly treatments the boy was healed, and the trouble did not recur.

To heal a child is not difficult. If parents only knew how rapidly and readily their child would respond! For this is where spiritual healing finds no barriers of prejudice, of preconceived opinions or sheer materialism.

This young patient might of course have recovered normally and naturally without any treatment from me – although his mother declared that he had been growing worse rather than better before he received spiritual healing. His doctor's medicine might have helped, but in my experience drugs which dull the sensibilities of a patient prove harmful in the long run. I believe the boy would have become gradually worse; his memory and mentality would have weakened; his neck and shoulders would have become shrunken; fits or convulsions, caused by his etheric body slipping out of alignment with the physical, might have occurred. Long and rather sad experience would lead me to expect such an outcome. Let me illustrate this by citing another patient.

This time it was a little girl, rather pretty and winsome, who had suffered from fits since early childhood. On examining the child, the usual 'bare' feeling at the throat centre was apparent. This time, however, the trouble was of several years' standing. Weekly treatments were given, during which progress was marked; three, four, five, six weeks passed without a fit. I began to feel hopeful, seeing that before the treatment started fits had occurred several times weekly. Then, against all my advice, the mother took the child to a cinema to see a gangster film which terrified her, and she had a fit there and then. All the work was more than undone. It is a curious feature of this form of healing that when a patient throws away any benefit received, either ignorantly or wilfully, the healing power seems to be withdrawn from the healer for that particular patient. At least, this has been my experience. Afterwards I could do nothing more to help the child. The case was a failure.

Since then, during some thirty years or so, a succession of similar troubles (and some much worse) have come my way. These are cases which bring a heavy responsibility to the healer. They are more difficult to handle than purely physical complaints – if any complaints can be called solely physical. A healer needs to be very experienced before he is ready for these, and for what are generally known as obsession cases; though in any case nothing but good can result from this form of treatment, provided healer and patient obey its few simple rules.

What is obsession? Can a disease master and enslave the soul as well as the body? People can become obsessed by many things other than discarnate entities – by drugs, by overeating and drinking, by aggravated pride in, say, house or garden, by vanity of possession, or by their own thoughts and emotions. I also tend to think that people can become obsessed by the thought of a disease, become paralysed by the thought of it and lose the will to get well; even when they want to get well, there is no fight left in them. Strive as a healer will, nothing will induce such people even to try. It almost seems as if immobilisation of will power precedes or anticipates bodily immobilisation and the condition becomes an accepted fact. Can a surrender such as this be called a form of obsession?

I meant only to write about 'psychic' obsession, such as the two cases described. Occasionally this sort of obsession follows a fall (affecting, say, the back of the head or neck), fright or shock, and will occur either at the throat or the solar plexus centres. Many of my cases, however, are due to ill-advised attempts to develop psychic gifts by practising with the planchette, the ouija board, table turning or automatic writing. Very decidedly these are not for anybody to play with, and it would be well if their dangers were more widely known. These forms of obsession are curable, but they are not for the novice in healing.

Let it not be thought that spiritual healing is largely concerned with grievous cases. The majority of complaints are plain and ordinary, although some patients come along in rather a parlous condition. Even then they respond fairly quickly to spiritual healing, although this by its very quality makes a demand on the spiritual nature of the patient, which has to respond.

I have been searching my memory for a case which can be classed as typical – that is to say, no better and no worse than the usual run of patients, and therefore hopeful. My selection is a Mrs A who has suffered all her life from a damaged spine, due either to prenatal causes or to an accident in childhood (I cannot remember which). The patient was a little grey-haired woman, gentle in speech and (I am sure) equally gentle in nature. Her spine had a severe curvature, with several vertebrae partially displaced – as bad a spine as ever I had encountered. She was eagerly, even pathetically grateful to the various doctors who had treated her, and especially to an osteopath. He had recently given her treatment which had made her feel better, although she told me that of course the pain had never left her. When I suggested that perhaps treatment might lessen and even remove her pain, she said that she would be very grateful if anything could be done, but obviously had little hope. Having always suffered, she expected to continue to suffer. She was a sick woman, nervously exhausted by severe and protracted pain.

After the first of her weekly treatments she felt slightly better; after the third the pain left her and did not return. Two months later she was a different person, with a good colour and eyes sparkling. Her treatments continued for several months until the benefit gained was well established. The trouble in the spine should not recur unless she suffers undue shock, strain or illness. In all probability the spine itself will never be completely restored although the curvature will probably straighten out to a degree. What happened is that particles of pain in the etheric body around the spine, which had become almost permanent, had been loosened up and removed.

Massage can be helpful in a case of this nature for it employs the natural curative powers inherent in the human hand. Massage, however, is not on the same plane as the spiritual healing outlined here, because it makes no appeal to the spiritual nature of the patient. Possibly, for this reason massage failed with Mrs A when spiritual healing succeeded.

Mrs A may be regarded as a typical case in her response to spiritual healing, but not as regards her complaint. For there is no such thing as a typical complaint, but only an endless variety. One remembers people coming for healing with eye and ear troubles, with neck and throat troubles, with arm, lung and heart troubles, with spleen and stomach troubles, back and kidney, thigh, knee, leg and foot troubles; and a whole range of rheumatic complaints of infinite variety. They come, these patients, in succession, mostly feeling sick and sorry for themselves; they are treated; they depart, rejoicing, feeling better or restored to health. In this manner the work goes on quietly over the years.

Two more cases will perhaps fill in the picture more effectively, both being women in early middle age, both fulfilling useful and valuable missions in life. One had had pneumonia, which had left her with a sore place on one lung, and its threat that it might develop into something much more serious. Certainly that patch was there, tangible to the developed healer; real, and able to be reached by his psychic fingers. At once this healer set about bringing the patch to the surface and then dispersing it, a healing which only took two treatments, since which there has been no further trouble.

The second case was that of a woman with home and family deeply immersed in work for animals. This time it was internal bleeding – we had no definite diagnosis to go on, but the symptoms seemed serious enough to warrant a course of treatments. However, only two were given. Then it transpired that the patient had to go into hospital for an operation for a growth in the rectum. An X-ray photograph, however, taken just before the operation, showed no trace of the growth which the previous X-ray photographs had revealed – it had disappeared after those two treatments, and after some years has not reappeared.

Spiritual healing is both psychological, and bodily, the former preceding the latter. It is soul healing as well as physical healing. This is where atmosphere becomes so important – the aura or atmosphere of the healing chapel, the generally hopeful and confident attitude of the healers, and especially of the healer concerned. This cannot be conveyed through words so much as by the aura of the healer, who must not be intimidated by any disease, but face it with quiet confidence. There is no limit to the resources upon which the healer can draw. Behind him stand a concourse of spiritual powers culminating in the Master of all healing; whereas all that the disease has behind it is the fault or the sin of omission on the part of the patient which originated it. The odds are in favour of the healer. Why then are there any failures? Why do some patients make no response to spiritual healing?

Few make no response whatever. Some patients will attend for treatment with, say, complaints such as partial deafness or blindness which have persisted for perhaps many years. After two or three treatments, finding there is no magical healing, they break off their treatments. These are not failures, rightly regarded. Such cases indicate that their complaint had so far failed to teach the lesson it had come to teach. Illness in any form has always important spiritual lessons to teach. Often only illness can awaken the spiritual nature of a sufferer. If spiritual healing can help any soul in its extremity to find God – as it can and does – then no question of failure can arise with any patient. It is gratifying to heal the body; but possibly there is more rejoicing in heaven over one lost soul come home than over the ninety and nine about to take up their bed and walk away, so busy that they forget God.

What about those who become insane, the multitudes of people with unstable and unbalanced minds who throng mental homes? Are any of these due to obsession? Could they be helped or even healed were this realised and accepted, and spiritual healing given? All that I know is that we stand – writer and reader, priest and medical scientist alike – as children on the verge of a sphere of knowledge as high as heaven and wide as the world itself.

20

THE REMAKING OF MAN

There is no case of bodily suffering that cannot be healed, albeit the right conditions must be provided for perfect healing to take place. It is true that karma created in a past life has to be made good, nevertheless there is a cure for every disease, when once the soul is ready to receive God's life and power within its being. For then a transmutation of karma takes place, the soul having learnt the lesson its karma came to teach. In other words, the soul has at last surrendered to the Eternal Spirit, and in this surrender has received God's divine light and essence in full measure.

W.E.

Of all the centres or chakras of the body, that at the throat (where the neck meets the spine) is the most important to the healer, for it is often at this point that the free and natural psychic circulation or flow round the etheric body of man, essential to his health, is blocked or arrested. Such an arrest can be caused by a blow, by a heavy fall on the back of the head, neck or shoulders, or even by tight clothing worn over a long period. Trouble may not arise until years afterwards; it may never come; but should it arrive it can usually be traced back to its cause. A recent example of this was a woman who complained of catarrh severe enough to make her life a burden. She was some seventy years of age and bore a great lump between her shoulders half as big as a football. This lump had gradually appeared, she said, as the result of a fall; as her doctor was not able to do anything to remedy it she had patiently accepted it as part of her burden of life. The lump was still soft. It was obvious that congestion at the throat centre was the cause of the catarrh. Get things moving again, and the catarrh would be cured. So treatment was begun, its aim being to loosen up the lump and afterwards to clear away the released dead etheric matter by means of passes. Response was good, and within a few weeks the lump had been reduced to half its former size and much of the catarrh had been cleared.

Catarrh can also arise from the opposite cause – a 'thinned' aura at the throat centre. Such thinning can also be the result of a blow, accident or shock. Either cause becomes very obvious to the healer in the course of time; no one could fail to feel the locking and its resulting rigidity, or miss the effect of the thinning (not breaking) of the aura; for presently there comes an actual wasting of the bodily tissue at the shoulders and neck, and with it a feeling of unresponsive deadness over the particular area.

Treatment is usually successful. With a locked centre the healer can loosen up the neck and shoulders, sometimes working with a degree of firmness if the patient is not too old or frail. Gentle neck, shoulder and arm exercises to relax tension will also prove helpful. With the thinning of the aura, however, treatment must follow the lines indicated with the obsessed boy; that is, with the cutting of links, the working together or replacing of the thinned aura, the pouring in of spiritual light, and the final sealing of the aura.

The various centres or chakras of man spring from the spine, and (with an advanced soul) appear to clairvoyant vision almost as flowers, which radiate light and colour of great beauty. In the average man these chakras remain small and dim, so long as his being centres on the outer world. Nevertheless they provide the healer with an effective place of entry where he may pour in the light. For example, digestive troubles are usually located round the solar plexus. The spleen centre is also valuable to the healer, because weakness, exhaustion and debility respond well to an inpouring of golden light at that point. Many a patient feels sick, sad, loveless and lonely at heart, and his illness may well start from such feelings. In these cases the rose-coloured ray (rose being the hue of love) poured into the heart centre (situated in the centre of the breast) will help and heal.

The head centres too are important to the healer. There are such things as etheric pain particles. No matter where the complaint takes hold of the body, its pain and discomfort is registered by the head mind. A sprained ankle, for instance, may be very painful locally, but it is also felt in the head. In the aura about the head is etheric pain, and this is why every treatment should begin with clearing the aura around the head. Here is the healer's opportunity to pour in light and love; however he must *never* try to overrule by his own thought power any opinions held by that patient's head mind, however wrong they may seem to him to be. He will help the patient according to the measure of his own love, according to the degree of his own illumination.

A true healer can clear the whole aura through the throat centre – not by passes but by the power and light he can pour forth, which can radiate to any part of the body. He can diagnose any complaint, for he knows that in reality there is only one complaint, this being the soul's severance from God. If he can heal the soul, the body will be healed.

Much, of course, depends on the co-operation of the patient and his willingness to work with his own mind and spirit for his own redemption. This willingness is not always related to the amount of faith which the patient possesses, but depends on something more subtle and difficult to define. Perhaps the recounting of one or two more incidents will help us to understand. The first is that of a man in his mid-twenties suffering from asthma and also from eczema to such a degree that his hands and arms had to be swathed in bandages. His asthma was so severe and continuous that his speech was difficult to follow. He had endured these two complaints more or less since youth, but never before in so aggravated a form. Because of his illness he was out of work, but he had served behind the bar at a West End hotel for some years. This helped me to understand his case better. I judged it might be a kind of etheric or auric poisoning arising from his continued immersion in difficult psychic conditions. The eczema was nature's attempt to clear the blood stream, while the aggravated asthma was yet another symptom arising from the same cause. This idea was explained to the patient, who readily accepted it. He had been repelled by his job for a long time. He would do anything to get better.

Never was there a more docile and co-operative patient! With enthusiasm he entered on a course of molasses and yeast, together with herbs, to cleanse the physical bloodstream. He attended services in the Lodge and read some of White Eagle's books. Treatments were given during which entanglements were cut away, the aura was cleared, and spiritual power and light were poured in. After some months the patient's eczema had almost cleared, his asthma was barely noticeable, and his expression and appearance had changed rather wonderfully. Restored bodily health had not alone caused this change, which was due also to a process of refining. The changing spiritual vibration had made a new man, the rebelling nervous system was now at peace.

Here it might be argued with some reason that the man's faith had made him whole. Does this apply to the next case, a man between fifty and sixty suffering from a nervous breakdown? He had been more or less badgered by his wife into coming for treatment. On arrival he seemed rather intimidated by the general spiritual atmosphere. But I liked this man, and from the first I knew that he could be healed. Without comment I gave him his first treatment. He came twice more, saying that he felt better each time. Then he wrote thanking me, saying that he was now feeling quite all right and had gone back to work. He *was* all right; and I know he has been all right ever since.

This particular case left me more startled than the patient had been! Curiously enough, he himself hadn't been surprised; he had seemed to expect no other outcome. Obviously, his had never been a true nervous breakdown; his symptoms – chronic exhaustion, sleeplessness, indigestion – had been caused by some soul complex, by something going wrong, either with his home life, or with his job or his employers to make work hateful. So he had taken refuge in illness. Something during my treatment had set this condition right in his mind and he had been healed.

Another case, that of an older man with identical symptoms, had no such happy ending. At the outset I had no feeling that I would heal this patient. This was a real breakdown, brought on by overwork, which brings its own karma because nothing but a period of rest can repair its ravages. I gave this man three treatments without much apparent result. Then he went elsewhere, driven by that terrible restlessness which is a feature of his complaint. I was sorry, because had he bravely kept up his spiritual contact he would have been making good karma to offset the bad karma of his illness. In other words, he would have been healed much sooner. An interesting point is that here was a man who had long studied spiritual healing, yet when most needed his knowledge and faith had departed; whereas the other man, apparently possessing no faith, had been healed – because of some deep inner knowing. His had been faith of the heart, the other's, of the mind.

How these memories come flooding back! Here is a case about which I always think tenderly. The patient was an old lady whose complaint I cannot even remember, so long ago did this happen; I know that the combination of age and the severity of the complaint made the case fairly hopeless from the outset – although no case is really hopeless. Week by week the old lady used to come along for healing; everybody wanted to help her because everybody came to love her; but alas, she slowly lost ground, although she was never in pain. Her husband was a Harley Street doctor, and when she grew weaker he himself would bring her, every week, waiting outside in his big car to drive her home again after her treatment. Finally she became so weak that a healer had to visit her home week by week; she used to look forward to these visits. At last came the inevitable end, and our old lady went home to rest. Her passing was gentle and she had known little pain.

I shall never regard this case as a failure, only as a sweet and gentle interlude which is good to recall. How right it seems for one who was so beloved to have gone onward without shock or strain, naturally and happily, leaving no bitterness behind. Some lives draw *naturally* to their end; these are they whom spiritual healing can prepare for their passing, so that it is not painful, hard or protracted. Bearing this one incident in mind as typical of others, it can be said that spiritual healing by its very nature can never be wasted. Severe and occasionally desperate illnesses, can be healed, but if the treatment comes too late to heal the physical body still the soul body can be helped so that it is made ready for a brighter world to which it will pass gently and peacefully.

Now for two cases which illustrate some general principles and indicate what can be done for deep-seated complaints scarcely reachable except by surgery. The first concerns an elderly man whose hip joint had been smashed. As a consequence the top of the thigh bone or femur had to be crowned with metal at its joint with the hip socket. In course of time this caused much pain and necessitated a second operation which, although designed to set things right, failed to do so. After months of constant pain the patient was nearing collapse. The object of treatment was first to relieve the pain, the healer's etheric hands working to bring the etheric particles of pain to the surface to clear them away and thereby reduce inflammation at the hip joint. The second object was to heal the condition by the inpouring of spiritual light. This, by the way, can be directed right through a patient's body if the healer so wishes, passing from his right hand held on one side to his left hand on the other.

Although this patient was sadly worn by suffering, his courage was indomitable. After a few treatments he became so free from pain that despite his healer's entreaties he attended a garden party, spending many hours on his feet. It was a major surprise to see how the hip stood up to this treatment. I subsequently lost touch with this patient, who later became ill through overwork – though he did not, to my knowledge, have any trouble again with the hip joint.

Another case was of a woman in her forties suffering from a persistent and painful form of colitis. This again yielded to treatment, so much so that the patient, feeling very much better and full of vigour, embarked on a round of social activities which speedily brought on another attack of colitis. Afterwards I could do nothing more. Again, the power was withdrawn from me for this particular patient. There are invisible powers which work with and through a healer, and if the healing is frustrated or squandered, they withdraw.

Both these incidents indicate how necessary it is for the patient to conserve the spiritual power once it is given; and the first illustrates how deep-seated physical ills can be dispersed even where surgery has failed.

I would pay grateful tribute to the invisible powers which labour with and through a healer, for without them the healer will accomplish nothing. They are friendly, loving powers, ever ready and waiting to serve. They may not be exploited; they may not be dictated to – and they never dictate; they are dependable, ever ready to minister, and they are patient even with the ungrateful. Without them no healer can heal. With them – and in the exact degree that he is in accord with them – the healer can heal his fellow creatures.

21

THE REMAKING OF MAN *(continued)*

You cannot reach great heights in a day, nor yet in a week or a month, but only through constant effort in every problem that confronts you, in every action, and through daily meditation. By meditation we do not mean spending a long time in a chamber set apart, but by being ever mindful of the temple within you as you journey on your daily round.

W.E.

I now plan to describe a single healing treatment from beginning to end, in such a way as to indicate the method and procedure of nearly all such treatments.*

Here then is our average patient waiting to receive his average treatment for his average complaint. What shall that complaint be? I choose one which (so far as the healer is concerned) can be plain, straightforward and without complications – namely, lumbago, which offers a broad expanse of human back to treat, and can soon be cleared away. Our patient, let us imagine, has shuffled into the healing chapel, and with many a wince has seated himself facing the altar. He has removed his outer garments and has been left to wait for a few minutes, to let the condition and atmosphere make itself felt. Then I arrive, wearing a white linen coat. This is because ordinary clothes in time become steeped in the auras of various patients, and the white coat is washable. I stand behind my patient with my hand on his throat centre (where the back of the neck joins the shoulders). Gradually I become aware of the inner man that is there – of the amount and quality of his vitality, and whether he will mentally resist or absorb my treatment. All the while I am gaining contact with my invisible helper, I am becoming attuned to the Christ power, to the Angels of Healing; then I begin to clear the aura around the

* See also Postscript.

head, making passes through the aura, almost without contact with the head, down from the crown to the shoulders. Each pass is made with intense soul concentration, so that something is drawn away from the aura. Auric matter clings to the hands, but can be removed by a sharp flick at the end of each pass, off the shoulders when the head and neck are being treated; off the hips when the upper part of the body is being treated; and off the feet for the lower trunk and legs. This 'flicking off' clears the healer's hands in readiness for the next pass. Perhaps a dozen passes will suffice for the head aura. This completes the first stage of any treatment. The rest of the treatment can take many forms, depending on the complaint being treated.

Here it is lumbago. With many a protest our patient is assisted onto the healing couch (as high as an average table and with a fairly hard mattress and a pillow). Clothes, within reason, do not hinder treatment to any great extent, with the exception of rubber belts or boned corsets. Since we are to treat the back, our patient now lies on his face, his body slightly inclined towards the healer. Now is the time to clear the aura of his back, from his shoulders to his feet, with long sweeping passes, drawing away waste etheric matter. Sometimes the healer must strip his hands free of this matter – that is, strip the left with the right hand and vice versa – much as one might pull and shake off dirt or dust. The aim is to keep hands and arms as clear as possible, so that each pass is made with freshly clean hands. The aura having been cleared from head to foot, it is time to start on the complaint itself. Let the healer investigate cautiously. Lumbago is usually tender to the touch, although sometimes the pain is deep seated. In such case make a special clearing at this point with firm passes, flicking off at the hips each time. All this is preliminary to the real treatment. Now the healer has to bring out the lumbago itself by loosening it up. There are several ways of doing this. Mine is to work on the patient's back with my right hand (in healing the right hand gives out power and the left receives), moving it in small circles of about six inches diameter in a clock-wise direction, always with power. Nothing can be accomplished without continuous concentration – not a rigid knitting of the brow kind of concentration, but a steady, gentle concentration at the heart centre, a focusing of the whole being at the heart. With each circular pass – for that is what they are – one must will the pain to the surface. Lift it out by will power of the heart (divine will). Make a dozen or so of these circular passes; then sweep away what has been brought to the surface by passes with a flick off at the hips or at the feet. Repeat the circular passes, then clear away as before. Keep on until you feel that you have brought out some or even most of the pain. Don't worry, however, if the pain still remains. Lumbago may linger for a time.

Your patient is now ready for the next stage. He still lies more or less face downwards on the bed, although his body partly rests on one hip, so that the healer can place his right hand (the giving hand) over the seat of the pain. The healer's left hand (the receiving hand) should be placed exactly opposite the right hand. Now the healer must make his great effort, a spiritual effort. By a concentration of his whole being he first receives and then transmits the healing power through his patient. He should feel the power flowing into him like bright sunlight, and let it flow outwards from his right hand to his left, through the body of his patient. This should continue until such time as the healer feels that enough has been done, until he feels that the patient has been warmed and irradiated. He will know when to stop. Your whole treatment, from the beginning when you first set your hands upon his shoulders, should have had a peaceful, relaxing effect, so that now, when you help your patient to roll over onto his back he should have no difficulty in lying comfortably relaxed and at peace. You should explain to your patient beforehand that the process of healing continues after the actual treatment is over; and he should be encouraged to rest for ten or fifteen minutes after his treatment.

The patient is by now completely relaxed (let us hope) in mind and body. Now is your opportunity to find out the underlying cause of his lumbago. Let your left hand rest lightly on his solar plexus. Try to sense whether the muscular sheaths which should protect it are firm and taut, or are loose and flabby. Does that solar plexus radiate health or otherwise? The sense of touch (etheric touch) can help to answer these queries. The solar plexus condition is indicative of the condition of the body mind behind it. That receiving left hand of the healer can sense many things as it becomes trained. It can locate the site of a disease, the severity of that disease, and sense the patient's prospects of throwing it off. The healer can develop these faculties; but of course, they have to be earned by spiritual effort.

As with the solar plexus, so can the condition of the heart be ascertained. It is possible to 'feel' the heart centre in the middle of the breast, and to learn much by its response.

Suppose the healer decides that the solar plexus or the heart centre should be treated in addition to the back, how does he go about it? By pouring in the light, by centralising it on these centres. This done, the head mind (which can be responsible for many troubles) still remains to be treated. He must try to irradiate the poor head mind. My own practice is to hold my hands above the patient's forehead, and quietly concentrate my being on the head mind by pouring in light and love to illumine that wayward mind. This done, I quietly steal away, never forgetting to wash my hands after each treatment.

My aim throughout has been to avoid jarring, startling or disturbing the patient in any way by any sudden noise, movement or touch. It is always better, so far as is possible, to remain quite quiet during a treatment. The patient should sink down into a deep tranquillity as if the bed on which he lies is magically charming his ills away.

This has taken long to tell, but in practice everything can be done in about a quarter of an hour. It will require some time and practice to become deft and certain with the routine of a treatment. Therefore the healing treatment described should be practised by new healers on another healer, or on a friend, bearing in mind that any accidental bang or jar can spoil a whole treatment.

In all essentials, treatments need not differ widely. The same routine can be adapted for almost any complaint.

Is it necessary to write about the deep satisfaction, the inner joy which this healing can bring to the healer? Surely not. Nor need the close bond of friendship which can develop between healer and patient be laboured. These things just happen and they spell happiness.

We have been told that it is more blessed to give than to receive; we are also assured that he who gives will in due course receive back in full measure any kindness which he expends. In this way will God's blessing on his labours be made manifest in his life.

22

CONCLUSIONS

Try to realise that all the physical laws which govern the world originate from the spiritual spheres, and are actually spiritual laws translated into the physical; for the physical world is but a reflection of a higher and more real state of life.

W.E.

Perhaps it is good, when feeling harassed, to remember that all eternity lies before us to use and to enjoy. However, there will always be a hurried someone wanting to know why the ritual of passes, of pouring in of the light, and all the other directions for healing set forth in these pages, cannot be omitted. He will ask why divine healing is not immediately available in unlimited quantity for everyone, everywhere, at any moment? To which we humbly answer, 'Yes; why not?'

Whereon our friend will make the rejoinder, 'Then you should heal forthwith by the word of power, by a touch of the hand, by a glance, as did the Master long ago. If your methods are really effective you should be able to heal a hundred people where you now labour over one.'

To which we answer, 'We too are humbly waiting to see healing demonstrated by master healers, in this way.' Meanwhile, we lesser ones must carry on quietly, glad to do what we can. We shall realise that as far as we are concerned it is better not to heal too quickly; because by diligence and patience, by perseverance, by keeping on in faith, healer and patient learn to like and trust each other. Nothing can come of a healing where the patient takes and the healer gives everything. Perhaps it is good that patients cannot be healed all at once; that they must come for treatment over a period of weeks or months during which a slow improvement, probably culminating in a cure, takes place. This seems natural and right; a complaint which has been maturing perhaps for years cannot be remedied on the instant. Some afflictions, as Jesus said, can only be cast out by prayer and fasting. The healer will come across plenty of these; but in place of prayer and fasting he must expend himself in patience and humility. So also must the patient learn a measure of self-surrender, and a measure of appreciation of what the healer is giving. For it is a portion of life itself the healer passes on – of his own vital force, his own spiritual vitality.

People will challenge this, saying that as there is an ocean of spiritual power around us upon which we can draw; why should any healer become depleted? Surely he has only to open himself to become immediately recharged? It is true that there exists an inexhaustible ocean of spiritual power; it is also true that it can recharge a healer. So also is our world and the skies above charged with electricity. Yet the battery of a motor car can be speedily exhausted and will take many miles of running on the road to recharge. The healer too must allow time for replenishment. Then, far from being depleted, he should gain in health and well-being as a result of his healing.

How many patients could the average healer undertake to treat in a day, in a week? This depends on the patients, and on the nature of the complaints. When my own healing was nearly a full-time job, and I was in my thirties, my limit was four or five patients daily for five days a week – that is, about twenty-five healing treatments weekly. Twenty treatments would probably have been better. When a healer's daily work demands most of his time and strength, then to give two, three or possibly four treatments weekly will be enough. Some will doubtless challenge these figures, citing some healer they know who can treat ten, twenty or more patients daily; that there is no limit to his capacity to heal. Well and good. I write only from my own personal experience, aiming to set out a long-term scheme of healing in which the healer will do justice to himself and his patients. Exhaustion and illness can be brought on by too much healing as readily as by any other form of overwork. Be wise and restrained, healer, so that your work will be blessed over many years.

The experienced healer has the advantage over the novice in that he has gained a confidence, a feeling of mastery over disease. The novice is apt to be intimidated. The experienced healer acquires an intensity, a vibrancy in his healing, which only practice brings. But the novice must never be discouraged, he must work for the love of it, and be affected neither by success nor apparent failure. Let him also be wise, and not take on his patients' burdens and become emotionally involved with them. We are told to do no more than to help our fellow man shoulder his own karma; to pick up his troubles and carry them for him is to invite a fall. *Bear ye one another's burdens* – yes, but this does not mean anyone may heap his burdens on another.

A difficult condition to treat is exhaustion in any form – physical, nervous, mental, or even spiritual – that is to say, the exhaustion of courage, fortitude and trust in God. Exhaustion is no less karmic in origin than any other complaint, in that it has been brought about by overworking the body, mind or soul. What has been squandered by overwork has to be restored or repaid until there is again a balance at the bank of health. This is perhaps as it should be, but the healer can shorten the convalescence. What has been said applies to some forms of heart trouble, which can also arise from abuse in some form; for the heart is the centre of man's being, the sun of his universe; it is akin, in its spiritual nature, to God. A failing heart can be restored, recreated by divine power, when it turns to God devotedly and lovingly. God is almighty, all knowing, all wise; but He is dependent on man for his love and devotion. For man to surrender with love and devotion to God is to enter eternal life; for when God enters into us we become, in our essential self, eternal.

Meanwhile, let no one think that the days of slavery are over while any man is enslaved by his body; while anyone crawls around half alive, depressed, worn and hopeless; for this is enslavement in its saddest form – the lower self has enslaved the higher. When the greater self has accepted the domination of the lesser, obeys its bidding and listens to its forbidding, this is slavery.

But the higher self can always regain its liberty and take command, for it has access to consummate, incredible powers. The way to regain mastery is by a steady pressure of will back again towards health; and by mentally and spiritually denying every urge of the body towards ill health and incapacity. Quietly and sensibly must this self-mastery be re-established, not only over the body but also over its thoughts, feelings and failings. Shut down on corrosive, self-destroying thoughts. Entertain only constructive, loving thoughts, and put them into practice.

This is self-mastery. Coupled with this must be self-ministry. What is self-ministry? Are we not bidden to care as much for our neighbour as for ourself? Who then is our neighbour? Surely, our nearest neighbour is our body, which is also our habitat. None can be closer than this, or have more need of our care or forbearance. We should minister to brother body with wisdom, recognising and overcoming its shortcomings by self-discipline and wise living. This is the way to freedom from the thraldom of the body.

What attitude should healer and patient adopt towards the medical world? We have already paid tribute to doctors, nurses, hospitals and their staffs for their devotion, selflessness and service. Sometimes the burden borne must be overwhelming. Of course the patient must consult his doctor, who is also his friend. In any case there are a host of run of the mill complaints with which a doctor can deal far more quickly than a healer.

Moreover, it should be remembered that the spiritual powers can work through doctor and surgeon as well as through the spiritual healer, should the need arise. Nevertheless, things begin to change as the novice advances on the spiritual path. The medical treatment successful with the old Adam is not always suitable for the new. As the body becomes more refined and sensitive to the spirit, it reacts less favourably to ordinary physical methods and to powerful modern drugs. More and more as the novice advances on his path must he trust to natural ways both in his diet and for the healing of his body. He will respond to herbal treatment and remain healthy on a simple diet which would seem sparse to the man in the street. The new man draws light and life from the sun, from the earth, from water and air, indeed from God Himself. His body becomes an ever finer instrument, enabling him to live long and healthily. It is man's duty to lighten the burden of his doctor by using common sense and caring for the body, which is the temple of his soul.

To conclude, let the healer never think that he accomplishes anything of himself. Let him remain pure and simple, a channel only for a power far greater than his own. Only God is great, and is man's strength and salvation. On some days I see Him everywhere. To me He fills the bright skies, and the clouds are His raiment. He is the sun above, with all its warmth and glory giving life to man. The grass and earth beneath my feet are God laid down in sacrificial service, offering His body so that His humbler creatures can eat and live. God is a sharer in every heart, in every life, knows every thought and feeling, every hope and failing of every one of His creatures. Not a sparrow shall fall, not a hair go unnumbered. Everything is comprehended by law, the precision of which is beyond our understanding. Yet God is all-comprehending love, as well as all-comprehending law. God is more personal than man can ever glimpse, more needful of man's love than man can ever know. It is not our wickedness which is the barrier. God must sometimes smile at the sum total of man's wickedness, for it is mostly ridiculous. Ignorance is the real barrier which stands between man and God, and on its cross are God and man crucified. Then the pain God suffers can sting man to eventual repentance and so to resurrection. Then does he arise and go unto his Father.

How simple all these things become when we get some measure of understanding; for understanding is only another word for revelation, and revelation implies healing of man by God. God is the only reality, and our lives become full and real only in the degree that they receive Him.

POSTSCRIPT
THE WHITE EAGLE HEALING TODAY
by
Joan Hodgson
Healing Secretary of the White Eagle Lodge

Over the years since this book first appeared certain changes have taken place, not in the fundamental method of spiritual healing practised in the White Eagle Lodge (and now in the White Temple); but in the way it is applied and the organisation of the healing. The changes have come about partly as a natural result of the growth of the work. Briefly, the difference is that in those early days treatment took place as described in private, in the small chapels set aside for the work. Today patients are brought for individual treatment during the course of a service. The reason for this is twofold. First, the number of absent healing groups taking place has grown from the original two to more than thirty in the London Lodge and twenty at New Lands, the country centre of the White Eagle work. The almost continuous work of the groups, together with other spiritual work going on in the main chapels, means that a great reservoir of spiritual power is being built up and constantly replenished. White Eagle guided us to make use of this reservoir of spiritual power, to bring the patients into it for their healing. A form of service was developed, built on White Eagle's words, which by constant use has become a powerful mantram which helps both patients and healers to make a stronger spiritual contact.

Second, we found individual treatments in the small chapels, while benefiting the patients, seemed too often to deplete the healers; sometimes a psychic or emotional link would develop between healer and patient which drained the healer of psychic force so that he too soon became in need of healing in order to cut these links. This psychic draining rarely occurs under the present system.

The patients are helped, during the preliminary service, gradually to relax and become receptive to the healing power from God. They focus their whole being on the Christ presence, which becomes so real during the service that it is felt almost as the physical sun shining upon the participants.

At a certain point in the service the patients are led forward to stools set before the altar and the healers quietly come to them. The treatment is given in an atmosphere of absolute peace and silence, and everyone present is conscious in varying degrees of the beautiful blessing which enfolds the work. It is not difficult to picture the angels whose presence is invoked, or the shining form of the Great Healer in their midst, so full of light, tender compassion and divine strength. Plenty of time is allowed for each healer to complete the prescribed treatment and for the patients to relax and absorb the healing rays. At the end of their treatment, the patients quietly return to their seats and another group comes forward.

In the Temple, provided that enough healers are present, we can treat eight patients at a time. Usually there are two sittings but sometimes we have up to a maximum of four, though we try to avoid this if possible as it obviously entails rather a long sit for some of the patients. The ideal is probably two sessions, which gives sufficient time for everyone present to absorb the heavenly outpouring which seems to descend on the group. This above all is what makes the group contact healing such a memorable experience both for healers and patients. The healers, working as a loving group, seem almost to merge with the shining presence of the Christ. As in the absent healing work, all are trained to rise right above the disquiets of the outer self into that shining star in which the Christ self merges into absolute unity with the Christ self of his brother. From this plane of being the healing light pours down into the patients, awakening and strengthening in them that divine and all-powerful Presence which heals and restores.

It has already been shown throughout this book that the work of the healer, whether as an individual or a group, is to quicken within the patient that Christ life which is the source of all healing. In other words the healer helps the patient to heal himself. Experience has shown that it is much easier for the patient to come to this realisation in the atmosphere of the chapel or temple where others too are aspiring. As in meditation, each member of the group contributes something to the whole, and one is led to a fuller understanding of the Master's words, *Where two or three are gathered together in my Name, there am I in the midst of them.*

When the last patients have returned to their seats the service concludes with a prayer in which all humanity is enfolded in the Christ light and any individual cases needing help are silently named by the participants. Then, after listening to some quiet music, patients and healers peacefully go their way.

When necessary, arrangements can be made for private healing treatments in the Lodges. We also try to arrange for healers to visit patients who are bedridden, housebound or in hospital. Whenever possible however, patients are encouraged to attend the contact healing services as described. The results of this form of healing have been remarkable, and it may well encourage other sufferers, and indeed healers, to read in the following pages about some of the truly beautiful and sometimes miraculous healing which has come about either through the work of the absent healing groups, or the contact healing services.

Of course it is not easy to assess the real and constant help which patients receive. Certainly a large proportion of patients report that they are feeling much better, or that they have been given strength and courage to keep on keeping on in difficult circumstances, but usually they are having medical treatment as well, so it is difficult to know to what extent the spiritual healing is responsible for the improved conditions. Every month, however, when the reports come in we have one or two letters recounting healing which can only be described as miraculous. The following is one such letter:

'It is with such gratitude and joy I am writing to tell you the wonderful news that my visit to hospital for another operation is cancelled. The growth in my throat has in the last three weeks suddenly started to disappear and become smaller and smaller. It is a wonderful miracle and I am overwhelmed with joy and thankfulness.

'It was a very big, hard lump, and antibiotics and a blood test all pointed to one thing – another cancer. The doctor here was quite convinced that only a cancer surgeon should touch it. He was equally insistent that it must be operated on and the sooner the better, so of course a letter was written to the hospital asking for the surgeon to see me again.

'Then, whilst waiting to hear from the hospital, a matter of about ten days, I suddenly discovered the lump had gone down. I went to the doctor who confirmed that, though it was still there, it was considerably smaller. We waited to hear from the hospital and by the time the card came and my next visit to the doctor took place, he confirmed that the lump was even smaller than before. We then waited a week and I went again, and it was now very, very small; not quite gone, but from the size of a pullet's egg it has gone down to the size of a pea. The doctor has cancelled my visit to the hospital and I have to go to him again in three weeks to see if the swelling has gone completely. It is the most wonderful thing that has ever happened to me and my heart is so full of gratitude to you and your helpers.'

The following is a most interesting case since it demonstrates one of the spiritual laws underlying physical health. A young music teacher was suffering from inflamed or infected tissue behind the eyes, causing loss of sight. She was also a diabetic. The grandmother of one of her pupils asked for absent healing for her, without her knowledge. When the time came for a healing report to be sent, her kindly sponsor wrote to her, via her grandson, asking how she was and telling her that for the past three months she had been on White Eagle's absent healing groups. Here is the result, in her sponsor's own words:

'She [the patient] 'phoned me on Wednesday evening with the most splendid news. Her sight has improved wonderfully and the doctors are quite amazed. She said many times how very grateful she is . . . and I gathered that she wishes to know more of our spiritual truths.'

This is especially interesting in view of White Eagle's teaching that eye trouble is fundamentally due to a deep need in the soul for a clearer understanding of spiritual truth. The functions of the physical body are much more closely involved with the soul life than most people realise, although modern doctors are beginning to recognise that many illnesses have a psychosomatic cause.

Animals also often respond beautifully to spiritual healing treatment. One such is a pony Twinkle, aged twenty-three years, who was suffering seriously from laminitis. Again we quote the actual letter:

'Twinkle is so much better that we are able to start using her again, and the vet has been so amazed at her progress that he asked me if I'd be able to look after other ponies suffering in the same way!

'About ten days ago she sprained a tendon so the vet called again in passing; today he has just been and says she is fit to start work again, so I feel that you must be free to give others in more urgent need your time and thought. I do thank you very much indeed. The contrast of the very sick, immobile pony of a few weeks ago is amazing to many people, especially as enforced idleness had caused loss of proper use of the hind legs. Now she is remarkably lively for her twenty-three years.'

As we have said before, healing is given to many different animals, from elephants to pet parrots. Recently we have watched with pleasure the progress of a more usual animal, a cat. Julie was placed on the healing group because she was suffering from a painful eye infection and the vet said that she would lose her sight. As soon as healing started, her mistress reported that the eye 'simply poured with water, then seemed very much better a week later'. We have recently received the news that she has now almost entirely regained her sight in the affected eye.

Children, being naturally close to the spirit world, respond beautifully and often dramatically to the healing power.

We had a little boy on the healing because he was troubled by frequent styes on his eyes. No sooner would one stye clear up than another one would come along, and the poor child was in much discomfort.

We placed him on our healing list, and were delighted to hear later that as soon as healing started the styes completely disappeared and have not returned since.

Another relatively minor but striking case was of a badly twisted ankle which caused considerable pain and discomfort for six weeks or more. In the patient's own words: 'I was at the time living in the heart of the country, with no car, a young toddler, and a husband confined to bed with a slipped disc. In these circumstances rest and care for the damaged foot was impossible and the pain was becoming worse.

'Mr Cooke said "Let me look at it." He then gave a contact healing, drawing off the pain and inflammation. The result was magical. At the end of the treatment, which was quite short and simple, I found that I could walk without pain and have not felt it since – and have not since twisted the ankle, which I was rather prone to do. This happened some years ago.'

Mrs Z applied for healing for a neuroma – a tumour on the nerve in the sole of her foot. She was in severe pain from the foot and doctors could do nothing for her. She was given healing and after three months reported that the foot had improved and the pain was less acute. Her next report was that the trouble had not disappeared but was more bearable. Six months later she reported an incredible improvement. The tumour had almost completely gone. Exactly a year after treatment started she asked to be removed from the healing and sent the following report. 'I have had no trouble with my foot since I last wrote. It is better. Please thank all concerned for the help and thought given to me. Thank you.'

Mrs Y asked for absent healing for her daughter Heather, who was suffering acute pains in head, ears and nose, and was to have urgent treatment in hospital for her sinuses. Mrs Y wrote: 'I am very thankful and happy to be able to write and let you know that Heather has been healed. She telephoned last night and when I asked her how she was, she said that her headaches had disappeared and her sinuses and ears seemed quite normal again. She had previously cancelled an appointment at the hospital because there was such an improvement. I thank God and your healing groups for Heather's healing.'

The following dramatic healing miracle was experienced by one of White Eagle's healers working on her own. '. . . My sister phoned me in a very agitated state. A neighbour of hers, whom she had known many years, had gone into hospital to have a nasal polypus removed. On examination, it was found that Mrs W had an incurable cancer which would not only blind her, but eventually touch the brain, too. It was thought that an operation would relieve her for a while, and so Mrs W was sent home until a bed became available. She was fitted with a cottonwool padding around the nose and ears as there was a constant and offensive drip from the nose. My sister asked me to give absent healing to Mrs W to see what relief could be obtained. This I did daily, and about ten days later Mrs W ran into my sister's house in great excitement. She had felt an improvement in the head as if something was being dislodged, and then through her nose poured an absolutely horrible substance. She just let it pour from her into a bucket, and when it had stopped, all discomfort had gone, and there was no more uncomfortable drip. My sister advised Mrs W to see her doctor, which she did. He, in turn, sent her back to hospital again. The surgeon was utterly amazed. He could offer no explanation, but told her she was a very lucky woman, and discharged her. Within two weeks, Mrs W was back at work, and there has been no trouble since. . . .'

Another remarkable case was that of a woman in her late forties who had suffered severe migraines from her teens. Attacks were frequent, often coming once or twice a week; severe headache would be followed by double vision and vomiting, and every attack meant at least a day in bed. One day contact healing was given when one of these attacks was beginning. The patient already had a violent headache, was beginning to feel sick and had resigned herself to a day in bed. After the healing treatment she had no trace of the headache or other symptoms and was able to start on her normal day's work straight away. She was amazed, because of the length of time it usually took her to recover. Despite a period of intense domestic strain, the patient has only had one migraine since that healing (over a year ago as these words are written).

The following case also concerns one of White Eagle's healers – this time a lone healer who, in spite of her own illness and pain, never once missed her assignment to heal: 'I am sorry not to have written for so long, but to explain my silence I must tell you that I had a bad accident on my front doorstep! At 68, I am fine, but I have an arthritic left ankle – recently, this has given way at odd times without mishap. On this occasion I had a fearful crash – causing head injuries and a badly smashed left arm. However, I woke up in hospital next day in time to remember my sick friends and to link with my group! I have *never failed my trust in this respect* although, alas, in a sea of pain I fear I have not been as strong in thought as I would wish.

'I was nearly five months recovering, when my ankle gave way again, and I rebroke my newly healed arm. I have been in great agony, and have been unable to "get through" except on Tuesdays – my day for linking with my group. Pain is purifying, and I have asked that the Master and my dear friends and my guardian spirit will cleanse me, and use me in a new and possibly better way.'

On receipt of this letter, we held this patient in the light at the noon healing service and also wrote to her asking her to allow us to place her on a group, and commending her for continuing her own absent healing work, even when in such pain. We had the following letter in reply:

'Such lovely warmth and radiance came with your letter. I received terrific uplift and help, too, both spiritually and physically.

'The next day, I had my normal lone healing session, and I want you to know that towards the end of the session I myself received great healing, and was absolutely uplifted – a steady and glorious "other world" warmth seemed to be concentrated on my bad arm. So you see, *before they call, I will answer. . . .* I should now be grateful if I could go on a healing list for a month, that the smashed bones in my arm may knit, and that I may be given fortitude. I am not as tranquil in spirit as I should like to be.'

Six weeks later came the following letter: 'I was in very great pain when I wrote to you, but I do want you to know that within five or six days after receiving your lovely message the pain of seven months *vanished*! The work of integration and repair of broken bones is now rapid.

'With a full heart and grateful thanks to the Christ, White Eagle and Healing Angels, I ask you now to remove my name from your list.

'Bless you all, and bless the helpers – the relief is marvellous, and it is so lovely to be out of pain.'

Whether the suffering be physical or emotional and psychological, the healing can work its magic, bringing peace, health and happiness. Here are two cases which brought us special joy.

We received the following letter from a young woman: 'My problem is so very deep that I find it difficult to explain in a few words but I'll try.

'As a child I was always excruciatingly shy and found it almost impossible to make friends. This got progressively worse until, as a teenager, I developed a terrible feeling of nausea and anxiety whenever I went anywhere at all – social things as well as shopping or going to the dentist, etc. I've always felt a wall or barrier surrounding me – I have never had a really meaningful relationship with anyone. My teachers pushed me into going to university and I managed to get a degree in biochemistry, although every day at college was torture. I have had the same job for ten years since I left, as a hospital biochemist. This has been a strain, not just because of communicating but because I feel out of my depth with the work – I've managed to muddle along somehow.

'The doctor told me it was "just" general fear and the physical symptoms were due to my producing too much adrenalin. The psychologist told me it was "just" social anxiety and taught me the mechanics of starting conversations. Anyway, to cut a long story short, I became so isolated and cut off and depressed that I decided to kill myself – I think it was only the thought of my father who would be left alone which stopped me. Then, *thank God*, I heard of White Eagle. His philosophy has helped me enormously, I understand the reason for life now and I *want* to sort myself out. However, this thing still persists, whenever I go out I still get this nausea and my body and especially my throat is tensed up like a spring with anxiety. There is a block deep down in my soul somewhere – I don't know what it is – I only know it is very very deep and this is why I am wondering if absent healing could help. I really have tried since I heard of White Eagle, but this thing is so deep, I don't think I can shift it alone because I don't know exactly what it is – I have a feeling it could even go back to past lives.

'I realise, of course, that it may be my karma to suffer in this way, and if the healing is not for me I shall have to carry on facing it but I *know* if I could only be free of this weight on my soul, then I could really get down to working for the Lodge. I want very much to become a lone healer in time, but it is useless trying to help others until you have yourself sorted out isn't it?

'If you think the healing is not for this sort of thing, I shall understand, I know there are thousands of people far worse off than me.'

We replied that we felt the healing could help her, and immediately placed her name on the White Eagle healing groups. Three months later we had this report:

'At first, there seemed to be no change but then I noticed that I was living each day more for itself rather than worrying about the future all the time. I felt so calm within myself that I was able to take a good look at myself and my life and I have decided to take myself in hand. As I explained in my letter, I had been very unhappy in my job as a hospital biochemist for a long time but I just couldn't see any way to improve the situation. I was in a complete rut, I seemed to have lost interest in the job and was just drifting about wasting my time. The healing seemed to give me a clearer view and after much thought I decided to take a leap in the dark, give the job up and change over to a secretarial career – the idea being eventually to re-enter the hospital service as a medical secretary.

'The very day I finally decided this, a leaflet came through the door describing a typewriting and secretarial course which was about to start locally. I sent for details and it seemed just what I needed so I enrolled and am now enjoying the course very much.

The teacher says I have a very high standard already and she is confident I will make an excellent typist.

'Although I am unemployed at the moment, I am not in the least worried (very strange for me!) – I have enough money in the bank to tide my father and me over. The employment exchange hope to find me a temporary office job soon which should do me good as it will get me out meeting new people. I am a little apprehensive about having given up the career I was trained for but I hope, eventually, to use my medical knowledge again as a secretary – at least I would be useful to the doctors.

'I am so very grateful to the healers who have given their time to help me (a perfect stranger) in this way and also to White Eagle and the Brotherhood in spirit – I really don't know how I lived without the wonderful spiritual knowledge I am gaining all the time now – of course, I nearly didn't live! I still very much want to become a lone healer myself and as soon as I feel really settled in a job, I will write for advice about this. I think I'll know when the time is right. In the meantime, I am still trying to send out the light to people I know to be in need.'

The second case is a similar one, in that the trouble was again more psychological than physical. We quote the patient's own words:

'Last September I was introduced to the Lodge by a friend, when I came to New Lands for the Walk and Harvest Supper: I was so struck by the feeling of love and peace and friendliness of everyone there, that it jolted me a little out of my habitual feeling of depression.

'So afterwards I came regularly to the Sunday services, eager to find out more of what was behind this peace and tranquillity that I had felt, knowing nothing of the work or principles of the Lodge.

'About this time, there seemed to be a strong recurrence of depression and nervous tension (which I had felt ever since I could remember) and which seemed to be getting worse. There seemed no point in living then, and I felt no desire to get up in the morning or do anything, and felt I could not cope with life at all.

I used to go round in mental circles thinking about it, and many times there seemed only one way out – which I attempted a couple of times, and was miraculously saved just in time: I think now for some purpose.

'I had received psychiatric treatment for about two years, but all the drugs and electric shocks seemed to make me more confused than ever.

'At the Sunday services, I felt that I would very much like to follow what I learnt there, and be able to open up my heart and mind, but there was the great barrier of my lower mind and past life – that always got in the way.

'So on the advice of a friend I wrote to the Lodge knowing nothing of its healing work but just explaining the despair that I felt. I was immediately put on the absent healing lists, and I attended the contact healing services.

'I don't think I can fully describe the wonderful difference there has been in my life since then. I feel I have a real purpose in life now, and it really is worth making the effort and enjoying it. It has been a slow process and I know I still have a long way to go, but now I know that I have someone very close, guiding and strengthening me, I cannot possibly fail. All the petty little problems and worries, that were dragging me down, are miraculously being sorted out and gradually overcome, and to every day there seems a special reason for being alive and happy.'

A grateful heart helps to bring about miracles, as the following letter demonstrates: ' "Thank you, God, for all the help and healing I receive", is my sincere prayer every day, for I have had and am still having so much proof of God's love and healing power that to help others who, like me, have always had a dread of hospitals and a great fear of operations, I am writing about what happened to me last year.

'The two things I feared most came to pass, and I was taken to hospital to have an emergency operation, but I received so much help from God through his ministering angels that all the fear went from me. I felt so calm that even the sister remarked about it when she had to put the tube up my nose when preparing me for the operating theatre. When I came round next morning it was just like waking from a deep sleep, and when the sister came to my bed to ask how I felt, she could not understand when I said "Fine", for apart from being aware of the incision and tubes I felt very well. I also understand that they got very worried during the night as I was lying so quietly and peacefully.

'I did not know what had been done until the surgeon came to see me, and he too was puzzled when again I replied "Fine" to his inquiry about how I felt. He said, "Do you realise how near death you were when you were brought in? Another fifteen minutes and it would have been too late." They had had to do an exploratory operation, and it turned out that I had a perforated appendix, with very extensive peritonitis. The surgeon told me that I would be in hospital for at least four weeks, but in fifteen days I was out, and my quick recovery was a mystery to them. They could not see what I saw! – the healing rays that were pouring into me day and night. Also, looking out one day through the hospital window, I saw the clouds part, and there was the radiant figure of Christ with a shining being each side of him, pouring down golden rays of healing and love. An unforgettable vision.

'My hips are completely locked with osteo-arthritis, and there are very extensive adhesions in the muscles of my legs. According to the orthopaedic surgeon and my doctor, I should be in a great deal of pain, but I am not. This they cannot understand. Of course it is due to the wonderful healing I receive; and I can still get about, even though I was told sixteen years ago that I would be completely bedridden before I was fifty. Well this year I am a very young fifty-eight, and I *mean* "young" because of the wonderful feeling of light, joy, peace and happiness inside me, which comes from the Giver of all Life, our Father-Mother God. So I say to all, never lose faith whatever your trouble, for God will never forsake you nor let you down, and I thank God for being as I am, as it has taught me so much, and life is wonderful.'

The following beautiful experience of true spiritual healing was vouchsafed to one of our workers:

'Working in the healing department of the White Eagle Lodge, I suppose one gets used to hearing reports of the wonderful effectiveness of the healing. Although one is very interested in each individual case and deeply thankful, perhaps only a personal experience, such as I had recently, really brings home the full power and miracle of spiritual healing.

'I was in bed in considerable pain with a slipped disc. My husband and I finished our lunch, and he went over to the chapel at New Lands to sit in his healing group. I felt drowsy, so settled down as comfortably as I could and fell asleep almost immediately. As I awoke it seemed as if I'd been asleep for hours – a beautiful, light, refreshing sleep. I had the sensation that I was coming back from a beautiful place, and I was wearing a robe of rainbow mother-of-pearl colours; it was soft and fragrant. I remember a gentle blue, rose pink, a gold, and all seemed to be held together by a pearly light. I lay for some time wrapped in this rainbow robe, and in fact tried to go back to sleep again to the beautiful place! But I didn't, and as my physical awareness increased I realised that the aching and throbbing in my back had eased, and it felt light and easy, and somehow purified.

'When my husband returned he said that he had asked if my name could be called in his healing group, and I had received an absent healing treatment of soft coloured rays. I had known nothing of this, and indeed, in my drowsiness, had forgotten all about my husband's healing group.

'I shall never forget the reality of the "beautiful place" or those fragrant healing rays cradling and enfolding me as I awoke. This was the turning point after which I made a rapid recovery.'

Finally, a patient whose illness became a deep spiritual experience bringing her untold blessing.

'You may remember my coming to the White Eagle Lodge for healing and as I have just paid my last visit to the doctor at the hospital, I felt a letter must be written to you as soon as possible to let you know the doctor confirmed that the cancer had been completely cleared. He said it is a marvellous healing – and it has indeed been a wonderful healing. From the day he diagnosed the trouble, when he told me the truth so straightforwardly, I have received so much help both from the doctor and from those glorious healing services at the Lodge. My very deep gratitude goes out to all the healers, and all the White Brotherhood by whom the healing power is directed.

'In one sense it has been the most wonderful experience of my life and a testing of my faith in the overriding power of God to bless and to heal. There is the sure and certain knowledge that there is a purpose in all the experiences that we go through and a lesson to be learnt from each one. And no room now for any doubt or fear, whatever happens in the future. The memory of the experience with the devastating feelings of fear which came at the beginning appear to be wiped out. Only the sense of joy and deep inner peace are left. And I am no longer afraid of the word cancer! One is left with a wonderful sense of clarity of mind and a feeling that one is being prepared for fuller service and there is the desire to be more completely dedicated to that service whatever it may be.

'Did you know it was the doctor who suggested spiritual healing in addition to his treatment? When I told him about the healing from the Lodge he said it would suit my vibrations! It has been a great joy meeting him. I know he prays for his patients as he asked me to join him in prayer for one whom he thought would die very shortly; he just made such a lovely simple prayer. And after giving me a clean bill of health he said he would continue to pray for me.

'Once again my deep gratitude for all the healing power I have received. May all the work and the workers of the Lodge and that glorious new Temple be greatly blessed, and may the Light and the Love and the Power enfold all who seek to heal, and to bless all who come.'

INDEX